## Praise fo
## Growing up Colored in Cape Charles, Virginia
## Memoir by Tom Godwin, As Told To Metty Vargas Pellicer

Miles Barnes noted Shore historian and Librarian of the Eastern Shore Public Library for 41 years.

*"It is an important contribution to the understanding of the black experience in Cape Charles and on the Eastern Shore. The narrative is always powerful and is especially moving where Mr. Godwin speaks of his family and his faith."*

Marion Naar, Past President: Cape Charles Historical Society, Museum and Welcome Center

*"A most engaging memoir, at once intimate and universal. The book presents in his own words the vivid, moving life story of a sensitive, intelligent, and gregarious man through a period of great change for black Americans. Tom's long life and detailed knowledge of his own family history enables the account to extend from slavery times into segregation, the civil rights era, and the present day. Son of an economically successful family, Tom's description of life in a small segregated southern town is authentic and not without humor. Through his words one comes as close as would be possible to experience and deal with the daily insults, inequities and unfairness of life for a black person in a climate of unquestioned white supremacy, but within a town which also contained a vibrant and confident black community. The account is enriched by the author's framing Tom's core personal material in local and national historical context and adding observations from her own Filipino life experience. The book is a captivating read."*

Mary Barrow, award-winning author of "Small Moments, A Child's Memories of the Civil Rights Movement"

*The promise of our future is built on the foundation of our past. This carefully crafted memoir by Tom Godwin is a portrait of what it means to build a foundation. It is an honest portrait of Cape Charles, a small town in Virginia known as the 'Jewel of the Eastern Shore.' As told to and written by Metty Vargas Pellicer, it specifically traces the African American community's important contributions to the success of the town, a part of history that has been overlooked by earlier writers. It lays bare the joys, the accomplishments and the obstacles faced by African Americans as they built businesses, homes, schools, roads and lives that intertwined with their white neighbors. It should be read by students of social history. It should be read by the residents of the town and the state of Virginia. All of our futures are strengthened by acknowledging our shared foundations. It is a wonderful addition not only to the history of Cape Charles but also to the thinking of those concerned with the on-going disparities between the races.*

Nancy Dalinsky, former resident of Cape Charles, now in Brussels, Belgium

*This is your best book. It is professionally written, and the subject matter is very timely. It also puts Cape Charles into a historical context. This is my view about slavery:*

*Slavery is as old as the history of the beginning of homo sapiens. Even the ancient laws of Hammurabi, the Greeks and Romans so called democratic governance, King John's Magna Carta and the American Declaration of Independence addressed the issues of some human beings as being more equal than others.*

*It was what it was. But at the end of the French Revolution when the western world finally awakened and embraced the ideas of the Enlightenment (the right to dignity and freedom of every individual), then there is no more excuse for slavery to be part of any civilization.*

Odelle Johnson Collins, former Board Member, Chesapeake Bay Bridge-Tunnel Commission

*Thomas, my "over-the-hump" classmate and neighbor, has vividly depicted life for the Negro in Cape Charles during Segregation. Well done, friend.*

# Invisible History:

## Growing Up Colored in Cape Charles, Virginia

A Memoir by Tom Godwin

As Told To Metty Vargas Pellicer

BookLocker
Saint Petersburg, Florida

PRINT ISBN: 978-1-64718-724-8
EPUB ISBN: 978-1-64718-725-5
MOBI ISBN: 978-1-64718-726-2

Published by BookLocker.com, Inc., St. Petersburg, Florida.

Printed on acid-free paper.

BookLocker.com, Inc.
2020

First Edition

Library of Congress Cataloging in Publication Data
Pellicer, Metty Vargas
Invisible History: Growing Up Colored in Cape Charles, Virginia A
Memoir by Tom Godwin, As Told To Metty Vargas Pellicer
Library of Congress Control Number: 2020913062

# Dedication

Keith Ansel April 12, 1961-August 13, 2011

To Keith Ansel Godwin, my son who brought love and joy to our family and made us happy in so many ways. He gave so much and asked for so little and left us much too soon. We will always hold him dear in our hearts.

# Table of Contents

# Preface

I first met Tom at The Historic Palace Theater event sponsored by the Board of Trustees and Friends of the Cape Charles Memorial Library to celebrate the Library's 100th Anniversary, "A Cape Charles Century, Past, Present, and Future."

In the theater lobby, another community group was distributing fundraising information about the Rosenwald School Restoration Project. I had never heard of these Rosenwald Schools before.

According to the fundraising pamphlet there were 4,977 built throughout the rural South during the era of Segregation with seed money from Julius Rosenwald, a wealthy son of German-Jewish immigrants, who became the CEO of Sears Roebuck, Company. Booker T. Washington, a former slave who had become very influential as an eminent orator and educator, believed that education was the key to improving the lives of African Americans. He and Julius Rosenwald became friends and in 1917, Julius Rosenwald established the Rosenwald Fund and with Washington's guidance these schools were built with active participation and support from the Black Community to support the construction of rural schools in the South, pay teacher salaries, and provide books and school supplies. These schools not only served as models of construction but became symbols of the African American community's determination to fight for equality and the key role of education in that fight. In Virginia, 364 such schools were built and the one just outside the Cape Charles historic district, located just past the railroad overpass bridge fondly called "the Hump" by locals, was the beneficiary of the night's fundraising event.

Before the Civil War, it was illegal in the South for Black children to go to school. During the Reconstruction, when free public education became possible, Black children attended school for the first time. These schools were at the mercy of local governments for funding and were woefully inadequate.

From the end of the Reconstruction in 1877, until the early 20th century, the Supreme Court ruled that it was constitutional for states to allow segregation in public facilities. Jim Crow laws were enacted in the former Confederate states. These laws were intended to restore White supremacy and to disenfranchise Blacks, limit their freedom and remove protections won after the Civil War. It was evident that "separate but not equal" became the norm in practice, a continuation of racist practices in the South since before the Civil War. The schools were especially vulnerable, since many European-Americans objected to African-Americans being well educated, fearful that they would no longer be content to remain in their traditional roles such as field and service workers.

These laws were named after a character called "Jumping Jim Crow," a minstrel act popularized by Thomas D. Rice. By painting his face with burnt cork, black shoe polish or greasepaint, he created a cartoon character of a Black slave as a dimwitted, grinning buffoon. This image, among others such as Sambo, the happy, lazy, child-like slave, Coon, the Black dandy, the Mammy or Aunt Jemima, Jezebel and Mandingo, sexually voracious types, Sapphire, Watermelon, Uncle Tom, Picaninny, etc., denigrated Blacks for the entertainment of White audiences and became cultural stereotypes. The minstrel show became a unique American theater form, and its popularity helped cement lies about Blacks. These images, found in posters, advertising, theater billfolds, and artifacts that are now seen by some as collectibles, were so pervasive that they served as subliminal icons retained in the minds of Blacks and Whites for over a century, and still inform the racist bias of today's generation.

From the end of the Reconstruction in 1877, until the passage of the Civil Rights Act in 1964, Black lives were governed by rulings and laws like those found in the Plessy v. Ferguson case in 1896. This era of "separate but equal" was characterized by urban migration, violence, lynching, the rise of the Ku Klux Klan, the formation of the NAACP, Martin Luther King, Jr., Malcolm X, sit-ins, protests, and demonstrations.

Paradoxically, it provided the environment that fostered the rise of Black entrepreneurs, intellectuals and writers, and gave birth to jazz, blues, spirituals, ragtime, hip-hop, rock and roll and rap; musical art forms that are uniquely Black and American. What is defined universally as American popular culture is a Black creation that is the unique legacy of slavery.

So, I was sitting in the back of the theater waiting for the program to begin and this elegant Black gentleman sat behind me. As he caught his breath, I remarked that he could rest easy, he had made it in before the program began. As we continued chatting, his story left an impression on me.

"I remember sitting in this same seat during the Civil Rights protest era," he told me. "I was part of a group that was discussing strategies of integrating the business establishments in Cape Charles. I happened to be passing by the Palace Theater, and something possessed me. I just walked in, and, you know, I'd never been inside this theater, I had no idea how it looked inside, we were not supposed to be here. Blacks were not allowed in this theater then.

"I walked in, I remember I was scared, but I didn't care. I had no idea why I did it alone. I was home after college, and I got active in the Civil Rights Movement while in school. I was familiar with Rosa Parks and the sit-in protests. It was an impulsive act; the idea hit me, and I just acted on it. I was so nervous I just went into the theater, don't remember if I bought a ticket or not, just walked in and sat in the first vacant seat I saw.

I forgot what was being shown, but I remember how scared I was the whole time. My heart was almost jumping out of my chest. I saw it pulsating through my shirt, my throat was closing, and I could hardly breathe. My whole body was tense, but I sat there immobile for what seemed like an eternity, and the people who were sitting around me, White folks, all looked at me and moved away without a word but with that disdainful look that I knew so well since childhood. And I was alone sitting there, waiting for something to happen. I didn't know what. And then someone touched me from behind and it sent chills down my spine. It was Officer Willis Mitchell, who was patrolling the theater, the first full-time Black policeman in Virginia. He knew me, and I knew him, and relief covered me like a warm cocoon and tension left my body. He didn't say anything, but he let me stay.

"That was in the '60s. Now, 56 years later, I can come here without fear of being arrested and without enduring the humiliation of White folks avoiding sitting next to me as if I were dirty or contagious, but I will always remember that time."

After the program began, he was called on stage as one of the storytellers, remembering the past century in Cape Charles.

I had just retired full time, moved to Cape Charles and had become very interested in its history. I lived just across from the Cape Charles Museum and one day I walked over, and was instantly fascinated by the exhibit of video interviews featuring students who attended the Rosenwald school over the Hump, the school that I learned about from the pamphlet distributed by the Rosenwald School Restoration Project at the Palace Theater where I first met Tom Godwin. He was one of the students interviewed. "The Hump" became a familiar term often mentioned in the interviews and fascinated me to know more about how life was like for Blacks in Cape Charles.

I chatted with Mary Morris, who further piqued my curiosity about local history when I learned that she had been working at the museum for 12 years and had just celebrated her 86th birthday. Like many local senior citizens I've met, she liked to remember how Cape Charles was

4

in the early days. I then went to the library to look for books about Cape Charles and found a few self-published memoirs, but most were memoirs written by White women about their idyllic childhoods or were books from the perspective of White men. I found a couple of memoirs written by African Americans about growing up as mixed race, but not specifically about growing up in Cape Charles.

I later became a member of the Cape Charles Rotary Club and discovered that Tom was a member too. When he brought Juanita, his wife, to one of our monthly social events, I sat with them during dinner and afterward felt like we were old friends. Later, he was invited to be our luncheon speaker to tell about his experiences growing up Black in Cape Charles. He also spoke about his desire to write about those experiences before his memory fades, but he didn't know how. This gave me an aha moment: to offer myself to write his memoir.

I had no credentials as a writer, except for two self-published books, one, a memoir of my travels, *Hello, From Somewhere: Stories of the Roads I Traveled* and the other, *From Miman With Love, A Grandmother's Memoir*, written for my granddaughter. I am a member of Mary Barrow's Memoir Writing Workshop and of Expressions, the Eastern Shore Writer's Group formed after we completed the class, but I presented my ideas to Tom about how to approach his story and we agreed to collaborate.

I chatted with Tom to determine how we would present his story; I listened and took notes and reconstructed his story from what he'd remember on that day. I wrote everything down as soon as we finished our conversation while the content was still fresh in my mind. I then had him review what I wrote for his approval, corrections, additions, etc. I mixed the interviews later with historical information, research, and information from Tom's correspondence and his notes as well as additions from Juanita and other parties, especially his sister, Jennie, and Ms. Odelle Collins. The chapter headings revealed themselves as the work progressed.

The Covid-19 pandemic presented some challenges as we were prevented from meeting face-to-face and had to rely on phone conversations and email. This was doubly challenging while Tom was solving problems with his internet connection and at the same time that his phone was not working well either. I hope I captured Tom's essence and voice and his point of view in writing his story.

# Chapter 1: An Awakening

It is a surprise to me that I am not angrier and more bitter about my experiences of growing up Black in Cape Charles. I guess I have to forgive, but I shall never forget how it was like. It amazes me now that practically no one remembers that there were signs all over the establishments here during the segregation era designating areas for Colored and White, a constant reminder that you were limited in what you could do because of the color of your skin. And, the most damning of all, was the daily encounters with belittling acts inflicted upon you intended to make you feel like you are a nothing, an object, not worth paying attention to, best ignored and forgotten.

This attitude of the White establishment still exists today. By failing to acknowledge the presence and contribution of the Black community, which many deny as being intentionally racially motivated, the same attitudes of denigration and objectification based on the color of your skin are still being reflected.

My father earned his living as a building contractor laying down cement for sidewalks, foundations, and walls. He and my grandfather had helped build many of the buildings in Cape Charles and on the Eastern Shore. My father built the sidewalks of Cape Charles at its founding and they still stand today. He also laid the foundation of the Cape Charles Post Office. I knew that, and many of the Colored folks knew it too and it surprised me that his contribution was not mentioned among the builders and architects of the building by Postmaster Danhof F. Van Dyke, who gave a talk about the building in one of the Cape Charles Rotary lunch meetings.

The Post Office

There was a photo of the builders and my father was in it but he was ignored in the credits, as if he weren't there at all. It got me to thinking about the many Black-owned businesses in Cape Charles and their contribution to the economy and prosperity during Cape Charles's Golden era. So many of them are no longer active and will be forgotten if no one writes about them. Now that Cape Charles is having its renaissance, I am observing the same phenomenon, of how the Colored in Cape Charles are being overlooked in the recalling of its history. Because Blacks were classified as property, they were not given names and not recognized as persons with individual identities. They were represented merely as numbers among a slaveowner's properties and were counted as ⅗ of a person in every federal census through 1860. Our enslaved ancestor's stories were not recorded by the White custodians of historical documents and it was illegal to educate the slaves, so there were no diaries or memoirs or letters to discover from library archives or family possessions.

My generation still has information from family oral history about our grandparents who lived in the era of slavery. We are the last link to our ancestors. Our grandchildren will be so far removed from their heritage and our memory in the collective consciousness will fade into oblivion.

That annihilation of our existence sends a gut-wrenching wave of utter desolation that chills me to the core. There are few books written about or by Blacks in Cape Charles. It is up to us in the Black community to call attention to our presence by being alert to our representation in whatever is being disseminated in government brochures, tourist marketing pamphlets, newspaper articles, TV and radio shows, and local historical accounts.

Hopefully, other places in Cape Charles will attract the same restoration-based attention as the Rosenwald School Restoration Initiative. Places like the original site of Gray's Funeral Home, the oldest Black-owned funeral home on the Eastern Shore at the back of Mills Gray's house on 643 Randolph Avenue and Mitchell's Store on Jefferson Avenue, are the types of places that need to be remembered now before they are lost forever.

I hope to contribute by publishing my memoir so that future generations can read about these times and see whether the races have come together as equals in their time. It has not arrived after the Revolution with its lofty declaration that all men are created equal, it has not arrived after the Civil War and the Emancipation Proclamation, and, despite the Civil Rights Movement and Civil Rights Act of 1964, the races have not yet achieved the equality enshrined in the Constitution.

Thomas Jefferson himself held this belief in 1781 as the Virginia legislature was debating emancipation: "Deep-rooted prejudices entertained by the Whites, plus ten thousand recollections by the Blacks of the injuries they sustained, to say nothing of the real distinction Nature has made, would make it inconceivable to expect that Whites and Blacks, former masters and slaves, could live together in the same society without resulting in divisions and social unrest, convulsions that will probably never end but in the extermination of one or the other."

 Lincoln too expressed similar sentiments in 1858, as a divided nation moved closer to war, "There is a physical difference between the White and Black races which will forever forbid the two races living together on terms of social equality."

Both did not see an end to the division and held the belief that there is an inherent difference between Blacks and Whites and proposed the solution of separation of the races, hence the founding of Liberia, a country in Africa to be colonized and ruled by former slaves, never mind that most slaves had been born in the USA, their home was the USA, they had known no other country but the USA, and they wanted to remain in the United States of America.

Therefore, most opted to remain in the USA and as we all know, we have yet to find ways to deal with slavery's legacy. The belief held by Whites that Blacks were by nature, inferior found its legal expression in the separate but equal laws of the Jim Crow era. But, Martin Luther King, Jr. came along with a dream of true equality and in the years since the 1963 March in Washington and the passage of the Civil Rights Act of 1964, the US has made great strides in realizing the ideals of the Constitution by achieving legal equality. But the struggle for true equality continues in order to close the gap that exists in education, employment, health care, housing, and opportunity in the pursuit of happiness.

My grandmother, Candis Scott Godwin, was a slave when the Civil War broke out, and lived long enough to see her children achieve success and respect. After getting married to Jacob Godwin, a veteran of the 10th Regiment USCT, she moved to Cape Charles shortly after its founding, and here my father was born. She died in 1938 at the age of 84, before she could see me go off to college. She lived through the tumultuous period of adjustment after slavery and during the Reconstruction and segregation era. She did not see the crumbling of the foundation on which the principle of separate but equal laws rested in the Jim Crow era, that the end of legal slavery did not end the story of racism and that we continue to have the ups and downs in our quest for a bi-racial society that Jefferson and Lincoln could not visualize, that although the struggle for true equality gained momentum until a Black president was elected, the gap in education, employment, health care, and housing that perpetuates inequality of opportunity for Blacks continue to exist, so long as White privilege is not acknowledged and the will to control it is not embraced.

My father's mark on the town's sidewalk

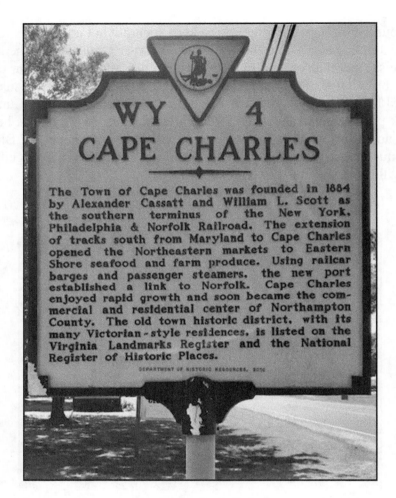

The Historic Marker

The Cape Charles water tower

Welcome to Cape Charles, sign on Randolph Avenue

# Chapter 2: The Beginning

My family was in Cape Charles at its founding, but you won't find our name in the account of Cape Charles's history. My grandmother Candis Scott Godwin was a slave until the Civil War. She grew up near Seaview, where she was being groomed to be a house slave. Her mother, Margaret Scott, was a slave in the Scott household. Her father was William N. Williams, a White neighbor from the Nottingham Farm next door. The status of a child follows the mother, so Candis Godwin's fate was determined at birth. She lived in James B. Scott's household and was a playmate to the master's children. She slept with them, ate with them, wore their hand-me-down dresses and learned to read from them.

Accounts about my grandmother stated that she did not learn how to write and that she spoke the slave's English, however, from our family stories, that weren't the case. She would have been careful not to show that she spoke the Queen's English and that she could write for writing, unlike reading, would have let anyone know about her knowledge. In the days of slavery, it was illegal for Blacks to obtain an education. "The White folks didn't want you to learn," my grandmother often told us.

Candis Godwin was interviewed by northern White journalists as part of the government efforts to document the personal experience of slavery. Her interview was in the Library of Congress Archives and often cited by journalists, writers, and researchers. One journalist, Kellee Blake even gave a lecture at Kerr Place. She researched and wrote a stage play about Candis Godwin's life and the lives of three other women. "Stronger Than Steel: Civil War Voices of Eastern

Shore Women" was performed in the summer of 2016 at the North Street Playhouse in Onancock, in collaboration with the Eastern Shore Community College and the Historical Society of the Eastern Shore. Candis Godwin was presented as the brave enslaved girl from Seaview who took imperiled trips past Union soldiers.

My grandmother depicted her enslavement as follows: "Massa Scott, my White people was good to me. Even when they got mad with us, they didn't beat us. I never had a whipping in my life."

However, she could describe in detail how others were treated: "They used to take that cowhide and cut 'em till their backs bleed, some just like to see blood run an 'they were not supposed to cry out except to plead o 'pray!"

Perhaps my grandmother's experience of slavery allowed her some advantage that others were denied after the Civil War, for many continued to live in poverty and though legally free, remained illiterate and indentured to the land.

My grandfather Jacob Godwin, Jr. of Savages Neck and a veteran of the 10th Regiment USCT, recalled that he noticed my grandmother one Sunday at the African Baptist Church in Cheriton, and my grandmother concurred, "I noticed him too, looking from the corner of my eye, but I pretended not to see him, but he kept on sliding towards me until finally he came close and held my hand."

That was how they met, and they got married on October 14, 1878. My grandmother liked to tell the story and she'd beam with pleasure as she recalled that they were told to be the prettiest couple on the Shore on their wedding day. After marriage, they lived with other family members in Capeville. Hearing about employment opportunities, they moved to Cape Charles in 1884, a year after its founding where my grandfather worked as a hostler, a horse handler, in the rapidly developing railroad town and ferry terminal.

My grandparents lived on 600 Mason Avenue where my father, one of several children, was born in 1895. Although my father was one of the younger children, he helped raise his other siblings and he started working to support the family in his teens. I never got to know my father's siblings in life except for my Aunt Daisy who survived until I was in my teens.

However, on April 13, 2018, I had an incredible visit from unbeknownst relatives in England who were the descendants of John Wesley Godwin, who as a slave stowed away in a boat, presumably from Norfolk, to Ellesmere, England. Karen Godwin Rimington, one of his great-grandchildren, became intrigued about the family genealogy and did exhaustive research which identified her great-grandfather as the son of Jacob Godwin and Candis Scott, my grandparents, and that John Wesley Godwin was my father's brother, my uncle. The information she retrieved from her research of court documents and archives revealed the hardships and family separations that were so heartrending during slavery, but also revealed the resiliency of the human spirit and the transformative power of family in overcoming life's challenges.

With Karen Godwin Rimington

My father was 19 years old when my grandfather died of Typhoid fever in 1914, whereas my grandmother lived another two decades until her death in 1938 at age 84. My father was a widower after a brief marriage without children to his first wife, Maude Bibbins, who succumbed to tuberculosis. With my grandfather, he had a cement construction business and later supplied the burial vaults to Mills C. Gray, who founded Gray's Funeral in 1895, the first Black-owned funeral home on the Eastern Shore of Virginia.

Mills C. Gray had moved from Nansemond County to Cape Charles sometime in the 1880s along with his mother and several siblings. There were jobs available and opportunities for anyone who wanted to make his mark. Gray was a carpenter and helped build many of the early houses in Cape Charles. Through his friendship with another carpenter, Conrad Grimmer, an immigrant from Bavaria, Germany who was also a mortician, he learned about the business, and initially, he supplied trims for coffins and later was hired to pick up corpses that were shipped to the Eastern Shore for burial. Most of the dead were not embalmed since Virginia law did not require them to be. Instead, they required vaults.

My grandfather provided the burial vaults which subsequently were supplied by Thomas Godwin, my father, and through his association with Gray, he met my mother Alston Joynes, who was the niece of Gray's wife, Jenny. According to family lore, she was endorsed by Maude at her death, to be my father's second wife.

My mother Alston Joynes

My mother, who was fifteen years younger than my father, was educated at Tidewater Institute, a private Christian school, and enrolled in Nursing at Dixie Nursing School in Hampton, Virginia. She was fiercely protective of us, her children, and was active in civic engagement. She was very active in parent-teacher organizations, Prince Hall Affiliation of the Eastern Star, United Order of Tents, and was the first female Deacon ordained by the First Baptist Church. She was honored as a Living Legend by the 100 Black Women in Funeral Service.

She opened a flower shop as an adjunct business to Gray's Funeral Home. She also became licensed as a notary public. On her 100th birthday on December 17, 2011, she was recognized by Governor Robert McDonnell as a Centenarian of the Commonwealth of Virginia and received a Proclamation from the Mayor of Cape Charles. On January 19, 2013 my mother died. She was 101 years old.

Gray died in 1934. His wife Jenny operated the funeral home with the help of my mother, who subsequently inherited the business after her aunt Jenny's death in 1946. Today, the funeral home on 618 Jefferson Avenue remains in the family under my stewardship with my wife, Juanita. We continued to grow the business and on June 22, 2010, it received a congressional citation from Alcee L. Hastings, Congressman from Florida, as one of the historic Funeral Homes in the African-American Hall of Fame.

The original building, where the embalming and preparation of the deceased was done, still stands today in the back of Gray's house on 643 Randolph Avenue. There are no historical markers to identify this to the current generation. His house and business were the only Black-owned property on Randolph Avenue at the time. There was another funeral home serving the White community on 640 Randolph Avenue, Grimmer Funeral Home, established in 1905 that later became the Fox and Scott Funeral Home until 2002, and is now a repurposed elegant Bed and Breakfast, Alyssa House.

I was born in Cape Charles on March 2, 1938 and lived with my parents at 625 Madison Avenue with my three-year older sister, Jennie. I remember our childhood together as happy in a close-knit family and enjoying the socio-economically privileged lifestyle afforded by my parents who ran a funeral business together, owned a cement contracting business, and who were actively engaged in the community.

Because my father owned the biggest cement contracting business, he had several vehicles including heavy machinery to move and mix cement. The city council often called him to help the city in many emergencies where his vehicles and machinery were utilized gratis. I remember one night he was called to lend his equipment to tow a steamboat that sank in the harbor. My father did not get paid, oftentimes for these favors, but I suppose he was able to get some concessions in exchange. I grew up with our family being amongst the first to have electricity, indoor plumbing, city sewer and telephone installed at home. We owned cars and our house had fine furnishings and antiques. I went to formal balls in a tuxedo and was always well dressed. I remember our growing up years within our family and community as idyllic.

My father was known to tell humorous stories that you would not know to be funny until later, and he also liked to give people nicknames. My sister he called "Bunny" for the Easter bunny because she was born on Good Friday. My nickname was Snookie, though I don't remember anymore how I got the name.

My sister remembers how she used to sit on his lap and braid his long hair. She and my daddy were close. On school days, we'd be home around three or four in the afternoon, and daddy would come home at about 6 pm. He'd turn on our big radio, the kind that stood like a cabinet from the floor and listen to the news broadcast by Gabriel Heater. We'd run to him when we were little and sat on his lap. Sometimes, he'd pull out of his pockets a candy or some small treat for us.

Then we'd eat supper, and my sister and I would help put away the dishes. On Sundays, we'd go to church at the First Baptist Church on Nectarine and Madison, and after lunch, we'd pile up in daddy's black 1938 Pontiac and drive to our grandparents on Seaview, go to the beach and spend the day.

Sometimes we'd drive to my mother's sister's house, our Aunt Della Joynes Collins in Wardtown, to play with the chickens and run around the farm, or we'd go walk on the beach. Sometimes we'd go to the patch of beach in Cape Charles at the end of Washington Avenue, where the Colored folks were allowed, and we'd bring a picnic basket and play in the water.

We didn't question the segregation when we were little, we just didn't mix with the White folks. We didn't pay them any mind and they didn't bother us if we stayed in our place. We used to play with our uncle's White neighbor's children on Randolph Avenue. My mother had lived there with her Aunt Jenny before she married daddy. We played well together, so long as we stayed outdoors. We understood we weren't supposed to go into each other's houses. We behaved well, our parents were strict, the White kids and the Colored knew each other. Cape Charles was a small town, and our parents knew their parents, my father did business with them, and so we got along without tension because we were well behaved and didn't cross the boundary. We were aware of the different way we were treated, but we managed to minimize our exposure by staying within our homogenous community.

Segregation was tolerable when we were younger, it protected us from the daily indignities inflicted on us and it wasn't until we were in our teens when we had to deal with it ourselves. My sister recalled an incident when she went to this sandwich place, Getzel's, on Mason Avenue next to Wilson's. There was no one else waiting for service inside when she came in, but no one moved to help her until a White female customer came and immediately was able to make her purchase. My sister was upset and thought how unfair that was, and so she didn't step into the store ever again. That's how we dealt with it, we avoided dealing with the mean ones. We knew who they were and also who the nice ones were, like McCrory's, the five and dime store.

I remember during the sit-ins and protests we couldn't sit at the soda fountain at Savage's Drug Store, so our preacher collected all the prescriptions that the drug store was filling for our Black neighbors and took them to be filled in Virginia Beach. Soon, the pharmacist noticed it and asked his Black employee why, and he was told about the protest. Desiring to have the Black business back, he integrated the soda fountain.

My sister, being three years older than I, went her separate way when she started school, and then she went away to Richmond and returned home after graduation from Virginia Union College to teach in the elementary school at Machipongo. She got married and moved away and now she lives with her daughter and grandchildren in Lenexa, Kansas.

I met my wife Juanita in 8th grade at Northampton County High School. It was the first day of school and we were in orientation at the library when this vision appeared at the door and immediately, I was smitten.

Tom, six-years-old

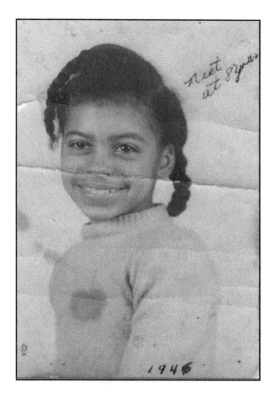

Juanita, 8-yrs-old

"Man, do you see what I see?" I nudged my friend seated next to me.

She was the prettiest girl I'd set my eyes on and I could see her now as clearly as how she looked on that first sight. She had a long dress and white shoes and her hair was long with bangs. Our eyes met and I stood up and walked towards her and introduced myself. Her name was Juanita Brickhouse. She lived in Hare Valley in Exmore, and she was in 7th grade. She was at the library to meet a friend. I don't remember how our conversation went, but Juanita remembered I asked her a specific question, which she thought was a weird question for a first meeting.

"What do you want to be when you grow up?" I asked.

"I want to be a home economics teacher, and you?"

"I want to be a mortician."

Our conversation was cut off when her friend arrived and I said, "See you around," trying to be cool as I could manage.

The next day, we found each other in the hallway, and soon, Juanita's friends began to notice us as a couple. I began carrying her books in between classes and we've been inseparable since. We started studying together and meeting for lunch under our favorite campus tree, which became part of our fondest memories of school. When the county demolished the school to consolidate the system into the integrated Northampton High in Eastville in 1966, we had a brick taken for a souvenir.

Under our favorite tree in front of the school bldg.

We couldn't wait to see each other every day at school. We were teased because almost everyone knew my family operated a funeral business and I was called the "undertaker" or the "gravedigger," which I paid no mind, and Juanita didn't get upset either, because we were in love. Juanita was nice to me from the very beginning and I learned later on that she thought I had nice manners, dressed well, and was different from the rest of the boys she knew. She also thought that I seemed to be busy and with purpose and she thought it was interesting that I carried a newspaper under my arms every time she saw me. She also thought I was funny, and I made her laugh with my jokes and sense of humor, and that I was friendly and approachable and seemed to know everybody. She thought I was cool.

We saw each other only in school and our parents didn't know about us until my mother needed me to drive her to visit a friend who lived next door to Juanita in Hare Valley. So, after I dropped off mother, I went over and knocked on Juanita's door and her mother opened it.

"Good morning ma'am," I said. "I'm Tom Godwin, may I see Juanita?"

It seemed everyone was occupied with some sort of chore, so I went to the field to look for Juanita myself. Juanita's father was a farmer and her mother was a skilled seamstress and tailor and also kept the books on the farm. Juanita was planting corn that day as her chore. She was barefoot and her hair was windswept, and she was as pretty as ever, looking flustered and embarrassed because she wasn't dressed for company and here, I presented myself in my pressed slacks and neat dress shirt and spit-polished shoes. Nevertheless, she was as excited and happy to see me as I was to see her.

Her father was out in the field, too, and I introduced myself and we talked for a while, and I learned later that he liked my manners, and had a favorable opinion of me, which made me happy. She also has an older brother and a sister, a twin brother, and a younger brother. I don't remember if I had lunch with them, but I had a very wonderful visit meeting her family.

I learned that at one point, Juanita's grandfather owned the largest farm in Hare Valley and at his death, the lands were distributed to surviving children, seven out of the original twelve. With other investors, her grandfather founded the only Black-operated bank on the Eastern Shore, the Brickhouse Bank. Incorporated in 1910, it served the Black community until it closed in 1916. Its building on Hare Valley Road in Exmore, was on four acres of land donated by Juanita's grandparents. It served as a community building after the bank closed and was torn down eventually. They also donated the land for the Hare Valley Elementary School, and the right of way for the street named after them in Hare Valley, the Brickhouse Drive.

The opportunity for Juanita to meet my parents presented itself at the debutante's ball. It was a grand affair, held at the school gymnasium, which my parents also attended. I escorted Juanita, who I thought was the prettiest girl at the ball, floating in her billowing pink gown. I felt like her prince in an elegant tuxedo as we danced the cotillion. Another memorable dress-up outing was the prom, and before we knew it, it was my graduation.

I graduated in 1955, a year ahead of Juanita, because I skipped kindergarten as I already knew how to read after my sister taught me. Juanita was an usher at the commencement ceremony held in the school auditorium with all the pomp and circumstance befitting such momentous occasion.

That was bittersweet for Juanita and me, for my graduation meant we would be separated. She would complete high school while I went away to Richmond to attend Virginia Union College. We knew we had to finish our educations, that was so important to us and our families since segregation was still the way of life in Virginia. It had been pounded into our brains that education was the way to raise our place in society and to improve our lives and the lives of the next generation. It was a scary and huge task to shoulder.

For Juanita and me, the separation of the next five years was difficult to endure. I proposed that we should get married, but she declined, saying that the time was not right, our parents would never approve, and we didn't have any money and all sorts of reality obstacles. But finally, I couldn't endure the hardship of being away from her.

I was in Philadelphia under a stressful apprenticeship with a mortician, and I felt it was time for us to get married. We eloped and got married on November 15, 1960, in a simple ceremony at my cousin's house where I was staying, officiated by a minister friend and without our parents' knowledge and blessing. I loved Juanita more for her courage in taking the leap and doing something so uncharacteristic. Love prevailed. I will always remember her, my high school sweetheart, on that day when she became my wife. She was luminous in her blue silk dress, and my heart could have burst with happiness as we made our vows to love and cherish each other until death do us part.

And so, we started our life together. I told Juanita I'd like to have a houseful of children and we had our firstborn, a son in 1961. Then, we thought a long time before having our 2nd, in 1969, a second son. When we had a daughter in 1970, we stopped, abandoning my dream of having a houseful of kids. I realized it was difficult with both of us working to support more children. I completed my coursework to become a mortician and Juanita obtained her teaching diploma and began teaching at Northampton County Elementary at Machipongo.

Juanita was carrying our third child when she had to resign from the county school due to employment policy of pregnancy as a job termination cause. She was offered a position at Cape Charles School, the White school which had been court-ordered to integrate both its students and staff. She was hired and given the task of developing the home economics curriculum. For a while, everyone in the family was attending this school except me, and so, not to be left out, I'd get on my bike and rode to school with Juanita's lunch. We were a happy and close-knit unit and raised our children the best way we knew how: giving them our love and encouragement. But, no matter how much you try, life controls its path whether you like it or not.

My eldest was taken from us sooner than we would have liked on August 13, 2011. We had just gotten back from a Bermuda cruise with him and his wife, Deborah Taylor, an attorney and another couple. Juanita had just gotten off the phone speaking with him about the cruise. A few hours later, we got the call that he passed on in his sleep. His wife said that he was fine, they had had a steak dinner, which he requested, and after dinner, he went to bed. Later in the evening when Deborah joined him, she found him still, not breathing. He was dead.

We couldn't believe it, we were in shock, our hearts felt ripped apart, like a piece of it was torn, it was too painful to bear. It was unnatural for a son to precede his father in death, but here I was having to endure what was not natural in the order of life. He was in his prime and still had so much to add to his accomplishments.

He was supervising the information technology team for the Department of Corrections in Washington, DC, he served in the Navy for nine years, received multiple awards and citations and traveled all over the world. He was fun and adventurous; he caught the travel bug while in the Navy and continued to travel after he left and invited us to share his love of travel. He was completing his studies to be a mortician. We buried him at home, and his widow after 20 years of marriage remains close to us and sees us often whenever she comes to visit his resting place.

Our second son, Tommy lives near us in the house my mother left to my sister which he now occupies. After a 2-year stint with the Armed Forces Signal Corps he attended Virginia State University and Eastern

31

Shore Community College taking up Information Systems Technology. He obtained certification from The Concrete Institute of America and OSHA and worked at Bayshore Concrete as a lab technician where he analyzed concrete for moisture, air content and weight. He lost his job after the company ceased operations. Now he's working at the Coach Tavern and occasionally helps me in the funeral business. I had hoped he'd be interested in taking over the operation, but I don't know. It is my hope that the business remains in the family for generations to come.

We were happy to have a daughter, and Juanita was especially thrilled since she would have a beautiful model to dress and pamper like a princess. And true to all our expectations, her life would have a happily-ever-after ending.

She was the first in the family to be born with complete legal freedom and full access to every privilege enjoyed by every citizen regardless of color. She is a thoroughly modern woman in her education, career, and personal life. It seems she personifies the woman who can have it all. Her first marriage to a TV producer, which took her away to live in West Palm Beach, then Orlando, Charlotte, North Carolina and Houston, ended in divorce after seventeen years.

But the births of her two children during their seventeen years of marriage conferred the title of grandparents to me and Juanita, a role that we cherished, and brought us closer as a family. We wanted to participate in our children's lives, and with my daughter functioning as a single mother after the divorce, we were happy to be needed to help. And we were also happy to see that the divorce was for the husband and wife terminating their roles, but not their parental role, and we are thankful that their father continued to be present in the children's lives.

And now, my daughter is happy again the second time around with her second husband, Perry Paylor, an attorney practicing in Silver Springs, Maryland, where they now live. Juanita especially liked the romantic way they met.

My daughter was in Atlanta on a business trip and while dining with her college friends in a restaurant, she ran into a former alum from Hampton University who was there attending an Obama campaign fundraising event. After many years of being away from each other since the time they were in the same class in college, they kindled a spark this time around and the rest, as they say, is history. We like her husband very much and he makes our daughter happy, so that makes us happy.

With our daughter, our lives have come full circle, for she has given us two beautiful grandchildren, now twenty and sixteen, who we adore and love so dearly it hurts. Their generation is so far removed from the life Candis Godwin, their great-grandmother, lived and my wish in writing this memoir is for them to remember that freedom is precious, but the legacy of slavery still lingers. True equality still has to be fought for, and we as a nation must not forget that there was a time when their great-grandparents were considered property and mothers were sold, separating them from their babies, husbands from their wives, sisters from their brothers and robbed of their identity. They were considered not as humans, but as animals. The only mark of their existence was a number in the plantation registry of property, all possible because of the color of their skin.

Tom Juanita Ansel Tonja Tommy

# Chapter 3: The City that the Railroad Built

In 1883, William L. Scott, the congressman from Erie, Pennsylvania, co-owner of the New York, Philadelphia, and Norfolk Railroad and a multi-millionaire "Coal King" purchased 2,107 acres of farmland and timber in Old Plantation Neck, for $55,000 from the estate of former Virginia governor and plantation owner Littleton Waller Tazewell. Here, Scott built a city from scratch to serve as the southern terminus of the New York, Philadelphia and Norfolk Railroad.

His partner was Alexander J. Cassatt, brother of the painter Mary Cassatt and an engineer who supervised the construction of the tunnels under the Hudson and East River and initiated the electrification of railroad operations. Cassatt dredged a harbor and designed the steel floats that could carry up to eighteen freight cars from Cape Charles, the terminus city named after the cape at the mouth of the Chesapeake Bay, across thirty miles of ocean to Norfolk. When the tracks reached Cape Charles in 1884, the trains from Manhattan pulled right into the terminal building where passengers continuing to Norfolk could get off the train and walk the short distance across the covered platform to the dock where a steamboat awaited. There were raised tracks on one side of the building where steamboats could "coal up" directly from freight cars.

At that time, the town was laid out in city blocks with roads intersecting in perfect squares, and already had a tavern, residences, several churches, a school, a newspaper named "The Pioneer," several businesses, and a volunteer fire department. With avenues named after famous Virginians and cross streets named for fruits and trees, it had room for 644 homes and a central park. The main attraction was its harbor, the biggest on the Shore between Maryland and Norfolk, "where the rails ended on the water."

The following year, on March 1, 1886, Cape Charles was incorporated and it quickly grew into a cosmopolitan city that aimed to transform the hostilities of post-Civil War America by bridging the intersection between land and sea, of southern agriculture and aquaculture with northern industries through trade with each other and the rest of the world.

By 1907, the railroad and harbor brought prosperity that nobody had ever imagined would come to any town on the Eastern Shore. The Delmarva peninsula, a long floating strip of land surrounded on three sides with water, which practically existed unchanged for centuries since the first Englishmen settled across the Chesapeake Bay at Jamestown, saw at Cape Charles an influx of people and freight that required the railroad to employ as many as 2,000 employees in its network of trains, ferries, roundhouses, ships, and machine shops.

Cape Charles, on the surface, seemed a city where everyone mixed amiably, where the first Catholic church and Jewish congregation could co-exist with its predominantly Protestant churches, and where Blacks and Whites could work together on the trains and shipyard. The narrative, however, would not be complete without incorporating into the story the Black experience of the Jim Crow South.

Jobs for Coloreds were limited to laborers and service occupations, such as cargo haulers, cooks, laundry workers, and cleaning crew. For customers, the ferry dock terminal and train station waiting rooms had Colored and White Only signs, which was the same for the water fountain, and although no signs were posted, a subliminal code was enforced in the booking of hotel rooms or eating in restaurants and the shops around town.

My mother, Alston Joynes recalled the indignity she had endured when shopping for a hat. Either she had to purchase the hat without trying it for fit or appearance, or, if she wanted to try it, she must wear a cloth over her head to protect the item from contact with her skin, which was not required of White shoppers. The taboo of touching the skin of a Black person is so demeaning and insulting and so pervasive and experienced from a very early age, that it affected us profoundly and made some of us feel dirty and ashamed of how we looked. The disgust of being unclean is expressed loudly in the taboo about drinking from the same water fountain or bathing in the same water, such as segregation of the public beach and emptying a pool and replacing the water completely if a Black person had been in it.

Segregation was observed in the city's physical appearance as well, in sharply demarcated White and Colored sections. On Front Street, which is now Mason Ave, where the White businesses and the residences on Randolph and Tazewell Avenue were located, the streets were paved and lighted with electricity, and indoor plumbing with water and sewer service were provided, whereas on Washington, Madison, and Jefferson Avenues, the streets were dirt and there were ditches instead of sidewalks on each side to catch runoff water. There were no water and sewer connections, so outhouses were part of the outdoor structures in back alleys.

Amongst ourselves, we also had demarcated a "Sweet Kingdom" section, where the more affluent Black residences and businesses were located, bordering the White section, and the interior, poorer business sections we called "Jersey," bounded by Jefferson, Strawberry, Madison, Washington, and Fig, where there was scant street lighting and things could get scary once night settled in. I was prohibited from visiting establishments that were considered of ill repute, but I managed to visit them anyway, unbeknownst to my parents.

Because Blacks were not served where White customers went, a parallel business community rose in the Black sector. This allowed many Blacks to rise in socio-economic prestige and the Blacks who moved to Cape Charles, from the upper Delmarva and the South in search of jobs and improvement of their lives, found their place in the sun, so to speak.

Eventually, travelers going north or south had to stop at Cape Charles to board the ferries and trains that would carry them across the mouth of the bay. With travel between New York and Norfolk shortened to twelve hours, soon, three roundtrip schedules were carrying both freight and passengers daily. Farmers would line up for hours to load their potatoes onto the trains and the harbor was the scene of bustle and industry. Everyone prospered but no one in the Black community got very rich, for in every step along the ladder of success we had to hurdle the limitations imposed by the White establishment to keep the Blacks in their place. We could only prosper so much by the permission of the White man.

My father had a contract for concrete work, but the White men refused to pay him his full price, saying things like, "I'm not paying no Colored guy that sum of money," and they could get away with it. They knew that my father would not sue them, and my father wouldn't because he would surely lose as the judges and jurors would all be White.

White folks cheated all the time and got away with it. The contract for cleaning the train cars and ferries was awarded to a White man, who in turn would hire Colored women to do the cleaning at very low pay and required them to work long hours without rest. Maintenance road work was supervised by White men who stood around talking while Colored laborers toiled under all weather conditions and paid low wages.

Even in jobs where they had equal responsibility, the Whites asserted their prerogative to rule the Black man. I knew a man who drove a delivery truck with a White partner, and in those days I already noticed the difference, in the color of their uniforms the White guy had White and the Black partner had brown. They were supposed to share the work, but the White guy sat in the truck while his Black partner did all the hauling and delivering. Additionally, White rivals in the business had no qualms in using sabotage to gain an advantage.

My father had a supply of cement in his storage shed that he obtained at wholesale, which he'd sometimes allow others to have in small amounts in order finish work on their homes, and many times he'd give the cement for free. The White cement retailer didn't like to lose any customer to a Black business so he sent a decoy on a Sunday to buy cement, hoping to trick my father into selling to the decoy at retail and then to expose my father to the distributor so that my father would be disqualified from purchase at wholesale price. Nothing came out of this, fortunately, because the decoy himself told my father the ruse.

The exploitation of the Black community even took on criminal proportions in the case of widespread insurance scams. Back in the day, a White door-to-door life insurance sales agent sold life policies to unsuspecting Black customers promising cash death benefits. My family was in the funeral business, and these Black clients found out that there was no death benefit money to collect when they were about to pay for the burial of their loved one. Allegedly, there was a failure to pay monthly premiums to keep the policy in force. Although the agent was aggressive in collecting the monthly payments to keep the insurance current, even taking valuables, such as antiques and jewelry from the insured when there was no cash available to make the monthly payments, company records did not show these payments. Apparently, these types of agents were pocketing the payments and not sending them to the insurance company.

My father tried to help the family by intervening with the insurance company headquarters, but the company could not cover the claim since the coverage had lapsed for non-payment of the monthly premium. The company did agree to reimburse payments to the other policies to keep them current, though. The agent was fired by the company but was not prosecuted, he did not reimburse the money he stole from the Black clients and got a job with another company where he could repeat the scam all over again.

These unscrupulous men also knew how to get information from banks if a check was deposited to their Black target's account, such as union wages or insurance settlement. They mounted pressure on the recipients to give them the money by intimidation or false information or would pressure them into buying goods which were inflated in price but of poor quality. These White scammers knew that they could get away with it because the victims would not win in court even if they prosecuted.

In the meantime, around the country, labor strikes were being staged and labor unions were being formed and the clamor for minimum wage legislation and minimum work hours were being debated in legislatures. In Virginia, the labor union organizers had to overcome centuries-old, closely held beliefs that dominated both employer and employee attitudes about White supremacy and the inherent inferiority of Blacks. With its strong distrust of change and abhorrence of intrusion from the outside that is perceived as a threat to the status quo, the unions didn't get anywhere in Virginia at all. Blacks tried to form their unions separately but were stymied in their efforts by lack of endorsement by the local White chapters to the national organizations to represent them.

And so, in Cape Charles, the whole movement whimpered and was no longer heard. The Colored section businesses continued to be small and geared toward providing services and goods locally to the Black community. But since the attitudes fostered during slavery still informed the thoughts and actions of my grandparent's generation, the Colored in Cape Charles kept to themselves and stayed in their place and went only so far as the White establishment would allow them and were grateful for the crumbs that they were given. And so, they rode the wave that reached their shores the best way they knew how, by rolling with the ups and downs of the tide.

Soon, the steamboats and ferries were transporting more and more cars, and Cape Charles at this time was a bustling town where everyone who needed to travel anywhere north or south passed through, where people of many nationalities mixed with agricultural products from the shore waiting on the docks to be loaded and the streets were crowded with buses, vendors, taxis, and touts. On holidays, cars were lined up in double lanes up to the town limits waiting to board the ferry.

World War II came, and the harbor became busier than ever, transporting military gear and personnel. It was bursting at the seams with Germans, Spaniards, Italians, Lithuanians, and Chinese passing through. When the ferries came in, men with names like Bootie and Sly hung out in bars, and the police were kept busy. Some nights, there would be up to thirty arrests. Locals going to the beach had to push against the crowds and buildings on Front Street. To relieve congestion and traffic, the railroad, in 1953, decided to move the ferry operations down to Kiptopeke, six miles south. Before long, rail transport declined as cars gained ascendancy and roads connecting America were built. There was a clamor for more efficient ways to travel across the bay and another idea as audacious as Cassatt's land-to-sea rail transport came forth: a land-to-land transport from the peninsula to the mainland, with a bridge spanning the bay.

Unbeknownst to the town, that was the beginning of its decline. In 1956, the Virginia General Assembly passed legislation approving an engineering feasibility study of the proposal submitted by Lucius J. Kellam, Jr. and his group to build a bridge across the bay. It had been Kellam's dream, the Chairman of the Ferry Commission, to build such a bridge after the Chesapeake Bay Bridge in Maryland opened in 1950.

Finally, in 1960, The Chesapeake Bay Bridge and Tunnel Commission, a group of ardent believers in the project, headed by Kellam, signed the purchase contract after all the hurdles of design, construction, and financing were met. One of the routes proposed was an east-west route that would have linked the bridge with Cape Charles but was dropped in favor of the Fisherman's Island and Virginia Beach north-south connection.

The Black community was excluded from skilled jobs created by this construction, forced again to work only as laborers and unskilled support services such as cooks and cleaning crew. In Cape Charles, the Bayshore Concrete Company was established to manufacture the custom concrete pilings for the bridge. Again, Blacks failed to get employment as many of the jobs available were immediately filled by White workers.

Once more, after it found itself off the beaten path when the ferry moved to Kiptopeke, the town missed its opportunity to march with modern progress. When the CBBT, Chesapeake Bay Bridge-Tunnel opened on April 12, 1964, the last ferry saw its final sailing as the cars traveled on the span parallel to its route across the bay, cutting the time of crossing from ninety minutes to twenty, and the distance traveled by land around the peninsula by seventy-five miles.

To superlatives and much fanfare, the CBBT was hailed by the Guinness Book of World Records as the World's Longest Bridge-Tunnel System and by the Reader's Digest as one of the Five Engineering Wonders of the World, earning it international repute and everyone's awe and wonder.

Even as travel increased along Route 13, with tourism being actively promoted by the state as it rode the popularity of the CBBT with marketing campaigns featuring its flying seagull logo, Cape Charles was bypassed two miles west of Route 13 and it languished for decades.

Businesses closed, schools closed, employment opportunities dwindled, a large population of the city moved, and what remained were retirees and widows. Property values dropped and the city's Victorian waterfront mansions could now be had for the price of an automobile.

There was excitement about revitalizing the town when the Texas energy company, Brown and Root, purchased most of the William L. Scott Estate in 1975. It included the Northampton County Golf Country Club but the rest of its development plans didn't come to fruition until Richard "Dickey" Foster came along in 1996 and began Baycreek, an upscale residential and resort Golf and Marina community, with championship signature Arnold Palmer and Jack

Nicklaus courses, a private marina, shops, and restaurants. The second development to arise from the original tract of farmland and timber that Scott purchased from Tazewell, it wraps around the town that he had built to serve as the terminus of the new Railroad and with Cassatt, dredged a harbor from the swampy marshes of the new town at Cape Charles to realize their audacious dream of a rail to ocean highway.

After failing to march with modern progress, first when the ferry moved south to Kiptopeke, and again when it was bypassed two miles west of Route 13 with the completion of the CBBT, Cape Charles, the "Railroad's Once and Future City," may still be realizing its future as it enters a new phase of development, where again its transformation is a renaissance that no other city had seen on the Eastern Shore.

Most of the Black population fled a long time ago, but the few remaining hope to make their presence felt by making sure that their story becomes part of the narrative of this town that was built on a dream and, with another audacious dream, may realize a future that the founding fathers could not even visualize in their time: that there will come a day when the two races can live together in peace, freedom and true equality as declared in the lofty ideals of the constitution.

The Cape Charles Public Beach

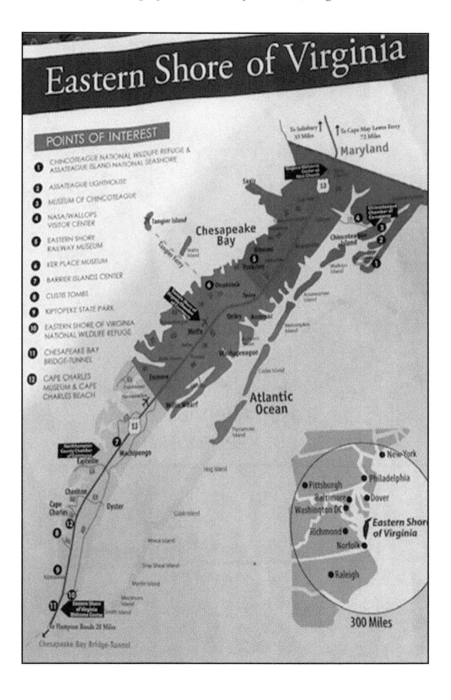

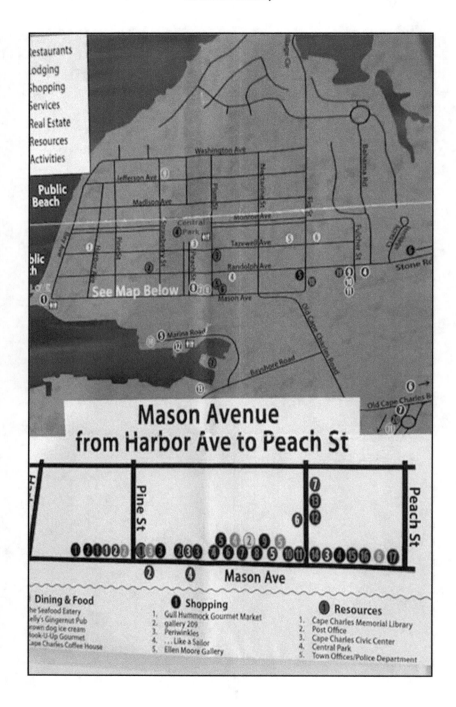

The harbor where the barge terminal and
railroad track met in the foreground

The marina village where the
old dairy farm used to be

The Pilot house from the ferry barge

# Chapter 4: On the Street Where I Live

Allow me to take you for a walk in my town in order to get a feel for what it was like back in the day. Let us start at 500 Washington Avenue. This was the former site of the first housing complex in Cape Charles: Gallop's Court, a nine-unit short- and long-term residential rental built by Bea Gallop, now the Bay Lake Condominiums. Just before we get to the end of Washington Avenue, opposite the condominiums where the Bay Creek Marina Village is now located, there used to be a dairy farm. They sold milk and butter right off the premises and delivered milk to the residences in a horse and buggy.

Site of Gallop's Court now
Bay Lake Condominiums

As we continue walking to the end of Washington Avenue, y'all see the remains of the pier pilings of the steamboat ferry terminal. They stand there like ghosts of dead trees rising out of the water. Imagine the ferries coming into Cape Charles Harbor and the passengers waiting on the dock to get on board for the Bay crossing to Norfolk.

Now let's turn left to Bay Avenue which lies parallel to the half-mile fine white sand public beach. The beach was only for White folks and would be crowded in the summer. Let's pause at the pavilion and admire the view of the town and beach from there. The original pavilion was constructed in 1922 and this is a replica erected in 1992 after the original collapsed.

Let's continue to the LOVE sign and the fishing pier which was built over the old government jetty. I remember us kids skipping over the jetty stones at low tide against our parent's warnings. As we turn left on Mason Avenue, we are at the Cape Charles Harbor, the largest between Maryland and Norfolk. This whole area would be crowded with cars trying to park, all sorts of people would be here trying to get on the ferry or the trains. When I had my newspaper route, I'd be here very early in the morning and I used to organize my papers outside of that confectionery shop, now the Brown Dog Ice Cream Shop. It is right next to where the Farmer's and Merchant Trust Bank was, which is now the library. I could go into the shop even if it had a closed sign, I just pushed the door. Inside, the shop would be full of Colored and White workers having coffee before going to their jobs in the morning. During the shop's regular hours, Colored folks couldn't sit for service inside. We could order food, but we had to take it out and eat it elsewhere. This is the shop where a White guy smacked me across the face and my mother became so enraged and told the man off.

Anyway, I used to hang out in the harbor and hustle for tips. During WWII, a lot of soldiers went through on the trains and ferries and I'd clean their windshields or run errands while they wait in line to park and they'd give me a dollar, which was a lot of money back then. I didn't tell my mother how much money I'd earned, or even let her know I did that since I was not allowed to hang out on Mason Avenue without an adult at all. The harbor and Mason Avenue were places full of bustle and activity.

The site of the barge ferry pier

The ferry dock terminal received barges laden with freight cars from Norfolk and connecting at Cape Charles with the New York, Philadelphia and Norfolk Railway that runs through the entire length of the peninsula to Pocomoke, Maryland whère it ties in with the Pennsylvania Railway and from there, the trains connect to anywhere in the country whère the railroad goes as well as to destinations all over the world. The freight cars could contain seafood and farm produce from the Eastern Shore, merchandise, military personnel and equipment, passengers, and hoboes. The harbor fascinated me as a child and I would hang out in the ferry terminal watching the bustle of pier hands loading and unloading the barges and when I contemplated the places that these freight cars would unload their cargo, it would take my breath away.

Let me show you the harbor complex next. It extended the full length of Mason Avenue, where all the buildings were on one side facing the harbor. It went all the way across to where the Shanty is and the Bayshore Concrete Company. The ferry terminal is across the library and the trains went all the way up to the barge ferry pier and the rail cars got loaded on the barge directly. It was fascinating to watch the maneuvers. The steamboats that carried the passengers docked at the north end of the harbor towards Washington Avenue. The steamboat ferries were luxurious ships that had restaurants, private rooms, and personalized service which the Colored couldn't enjoy.

The remains of the steamboat ferry pier

On Peach and Mason Avenue was Joynes Cafe aka Palm Tavern. Constructed in 1888, the building was first owned by Laura Lewis, who operated a liquor store and pool hall. Sampson Shawnee Joynes purchased the building in 1939 where he operated the Joynes Seafood Restaurant which was famous for fresh seafood, fried and deviled crabs until he died in 1983. The building has since been demolished, and the site stands vacant.

Did you know that the very first barbershop was built on railroad property right here by Albert Morris in 1885? It was a shack he constructed from scrap materials he found on the railroad yard such as car doors, boxes, and whatnot. It was located across the municipal building and fire station.

On 625 Mason Avenue, between Nectarine and Fig, Jefferson Grocers opened in 1884 as the first Black-owned business and first grocery store in Cape Charles. Taylor Daniel Jefferson came from Haytokah, Nottoway, Virginia in his twenties along with his brother, John Thomas to work on the railroad. According to his granddaughter, Evangeline Jefferson Perry, railroad work did not suit the small and slim Taylor so he and a cousin, George W. Henry started a grocery business. He became the sole owner after he bought out his cousin's share when they disagreed about the sale of alcohol which Taylor did not approve of. He married Mattie Kelp, a Hampton Institute graduate, and teacher. He was a community leader and through his philanthropy, the first school for Black children in Cape Charles was built on Washington Avenue. He was on the board of Cape Charles Baptist Church, Tidewater Institute at Cobb's Station, and of the Brickhouse Bank in Hare Valley. After his death in August 1936, his son, Walton P. Jefferson, continued the operation until the early 1980s. The building, a Cape Charles landmark for many years was demolished and now it is a vacant lot.

## The Kellogg Bldg/Northampton
## Service Station

We are now at the east end of the harbor, let's turn the corner on Fig and Mason and admire the Moorish influence in the design of this brick building which was originally the site of the first private dwelling constructed here for Mr. B. F. Kellogg. Raymond and Dorothy Spady operated the Northampton Service Station in this grand building for many years. They also offered a taxi and delivery service and sold used cars. There were several taxi services in the area, as it was a necessary transport system, for very few owned cars then. It was a reliable local service for doctor's appointments or emergencies as there were no buses except for long-distance travel and either you walked or hitchhiked on trucks to your destination. Raymond helped us a great deal in our funeral business by dispatching his vehicles to pick up bodies from all over the peninsula. My mother said of him in her interview for the Virginia Foundation for the Humanities when she was 96 years old, "He was good and smart and a good businessman, and he was just as Thomas George is to me, my son. He and his family just loved us, and we loved them." I continued my friendship with the family even after my parents passed.

Rayfield's Pharmacy

Across the street is Rayfield's Pharmacy, built in 2001 on the site of the Kellogg's Ice Plant, which was torn down in 1999, with its old-fashioned Soda Fountain constructed from its old chimney. The ice was essential in transporting seafood and produce on the trains, and before air-conditioning, Mr. Kellogg put ice underneath the rail cars to keep passengers cool in the summer. We never got to experience the elegance of train travel in those days of segregation.

This reminds me that travel in those days required careful planning if you were Black. On long trips, my father would hold extra gasoline in his car since you can't fill up just anywhere, very few gas stations served Colored clients. There was no Expedia or Airbnb to book our lodgings. We used the Green Book for guidance. Or, when people traveled to a strange city, they went to the Black preacher or the local house of a member of the Masonic Lodge or Eastern Star for information about lodgings. My mother as well as others had given lodgings to teachers, travelers, the postmaster accompanying the mail on the train, and hoboes. We communicated by visiting each other face-to-face. Not everybody had phones, and for a death notice, I used to put a funeral wreath on doors to let the town know about a death. People knew one another and took care of each other. Sadly, that is no longer true.

Let us continue to Randolph Avenue and Fig Street where Kim Starr has her Realty office now. That used to be a Gas Service Station operated by Oliver Joynes, Sr. He had a brother who we called "Do-Tell" and Oliver, "Olive Boy." We liked to give each other nicknames and many get to be known by their nicknames only. He also had a car repair business in the two-door garage attached to it and operated a taxi business, too.

Joynes Gas Service Station, now
Kim Starr Realty

My maternal grandmother sold fresh tomatoes, vegetables, and other produce from their farm in Seaview. She'd come down and park her truck starting on Randolph and move on to Tazewell. The White folks just loved her fresh products and would look out for her on the street and buy everything and she'd run out of her supply before she could get to the Colored section.

Grandma Joynes selling farm produce from her
Truck with me and sister Jennie

Let's continue on Randolph Avenue going west, here's old Mills Gray's house on #640 under new ownership. If you look at the back there'as a separate structure, that was the site of Gray's Funeral Home before my father moved it to 618 Jefferson after my mother inherited it from her aunt Jenny. The structure is historic, it is the oldest Black-owned funeral home on the Eastern Shore, established in 1895. I pray that there will be interest to preserve the building and restore the contents as a museum.

Original Gray's Funeral Home on Randolph Ave.

Let's continue on Randolph to Strawberry Street, before we get to the corner here's Denise Bland's office on the left, an attorney, the last door in this building that is part of the Palace Theater complex.

If we go left for Mason Avenue, the corner was the old Savage Drug Store, now the Lemon Tree Art Gallery, and next door to it is the Art Deco Palace Theater. Across on the opposite corner is the Altitude Art Gallery, which was the Wilson's Department Store, the most elegant department store on the Eastern Shore in my day. But these establishments were for White people and I seldom visited them when I was little.

If we continue on Mason again since we're here, the shops here were very often visited and sold expensive items. Cape Charles Coffee House used to be another department store with chandeliers and stuff. It would get very crowded here with shoppers and travelers with the Harbor across and cars would be lined up all the way to Stone Road.

Did I point out the "Hump?" It is the railroad overpass bridge to Old Cape Charles Road. It leads to the Cape Charles Colored School, a

Rosenwald School in disrepair after the city sold it to a seafood processing company after Northampton County consolidated its schools for Integration. It has been rescued for restoration as a historic landmark.

The Hump

Opposite "the Hump" is Nectarine Street. Let's get on it towards Tazewell Avenue and turn left to 629 Tazewell Avenue, the "Honeysuckle Lodge," former residence of successive railroad superintendents, which became the home of Thomas Dixon, Jr., the New York minister who wrote the infamous "The Clansman" which became a best seller in 1905. He lived in Cape Charles only for two years, from 1894 to 1896, but was promptly elected to the City Council for two years and became part-owner of the town newspaper "The Headlight."

Honeysuckle Lodge

He made a stage adaptation of the book which played to a packed audience in Cape Charles in 1908, requiring special runs of the train to transport audiences from all over the Eastern Shore. In 1915, the book became the basis of a blockbuster silent movie by D.W. Griffith, "Birth of A Nation". Its Eastern Shore premiere was held in 1917 at the Strand Theater in Nassawadox. When he returned to Cape Charles in 1933, he was already a renowned lecturer and gave his standing-room-only lecture at the high school, "This Country of Ours." "The Clansman" glorified the Ku Klux Klan and many of his writings expressed his belief about White supremacy. Blacks were not present as audience members at any of these events but may have heard about it from Blacks who were serving in the various venues.

Before my time, I learned about the activities of the Klan in Cape Charles by listening to the stories of the old-timers. I learned from them that one of the four women who worked in the cleaning service on Madison and Plum, in what was later Twilight Hall, either Mattie Clark, Mary Spady, Estelle Nottingham or Baby Boo (Dorothy Sanders), found a list of Cape Charles Ku Klux Klan members in the pocket of a client's trousers being prepared for laundry. Further, it was recalled that on November 1, 1924, there was a meeting of the Klan in the residence of the cleaning service owner. Also, they were recruiting members, and later there was an initiation and costumed parade of 60 hooded Klansmen at Central Park with about 150-200 spectators. They burned a cross on Jefferson and Peach and when the Blacks came out with guns to drive the perpetrators of the burning away, the Klan threatened to return but never did come back.

Then in 2019, the sheriff began receiving reports from citizens all over the shore from Chincoteague to Cape Charles that at around 6 p.m., Saturday, March 30," suspicious zip lock bags containing birdseed as weight and small pieces of paper that had verbiage depicting hate propaganda" were thrown randomly from a pick-up truck into people's yards. The bag contaied recruiting and racial hate material associated with the Loyal White Knights of the Ku Klux Klan of Pelham, North Carolina. I would not be surprised if there are local members of the Klan here today.

Anyway, let's continue on Tazewell Avenue to Strawberry Street, then make a right. Imagine checking out Mr. Nelson Nottingham's shop, an accomplished tailor who trained at Hampton Institute. Originally from Cheapside, he was the brother of John Walter Nottingham who became a premier builder on the Eastern Shore and with his brother-in-law, Robert L. Smith remodeled the New Allen AME Church in Franktown, Virginia. His sister, Mary Nottingham Smith, was a prominent educator.

On the opposite corner on Strawberry and Randolph is the post office, a proud Colonial Revival style presence which in earlier times housed the customs office and the marble showers. Y'all remember, my father laid the concrete foundation of the building and did the surrounding sidewalks, where many sections still stand and if you look, y'all find my father's name inscribed on the concrete pavement.

Next is the Big Elephant Building, behind the post office. On the first level, let us imagine the pool room and restaurant owned by Marion V. Dix. His cook was Grace Savage, Zamora Bailey's mother, who earlier operated Grace Savage's Place, a restaurant on Strawberry Street. Mr. Dix also operated a jitney bus service that charged 25 cents between Cape Charles and Bayview. Next door let's peek into who is having a hot shave at Sample's Barber Shop, which replaced the shop operated by Peter J. Finney in the building, now operated by Paul and Johnny Sample after their father Lloyd T. Sample who founded the shop in 1904, died. Alas, these structures are gone and all we see are empty lots now. But let me tell you about the Samples.

Johnny Sample married Evelyn Robinson who were the parents of John B. "Happy" Sample, who I remember well as he was our neighbor. He was born in Cape Charles in 1937, a year older than me and we attended the segregated Cape Charles School and Northampton County High School. We hung out occasionally when we were kids and we were kidding around in the pavilion on the beach one day, and the police came. We all scrambled away, but Johnny refused to run so he got caught. We were not supposed to occupy the pavilion, but we were reckless and did not heed our parents' warnings. Anyway, Johnny was fined $5 after he was caught, but he went on to become famous later. Five dollars was a big amount in those days when a laborer earned only $1.75 a day, so his father probably paid Happy's fine.

For eleven years, he played professional football for the Baltimore Colts, Pittsburg Steelers, Washington Redskins, and New York Jets. He was a rookie in 1958, playing defensive back for the Baltimore Colts that beat the New York Giants for the NFL title that year. After he retired from football, he played tennis in the senior age group and supported Black female players, and later officiated at Wimbledon, the

US Open, and the French Open. He also testified in a federal grand jury investigation alleging blackballing by the league due to racial discrimination. He wrote about this subject in his book, "Confessions of a Dirty Ballplayer"

Two bootblacks, Russell Wilkins and Colin Morris, worked inside the Samples barbershop. Later, the barbershop moved from the Big Elephant across the Street to 309 Jefferson Avenue. After Paul Sample retired due to illness, William "Willie" Collins continued the operation with Irving Jackson assisting part-time. Willie retired in 2011 and Thomas Wilson, Jr., grandson of Herman Edmonds kept the shop open until 2014, after which the shop was sold and renovated to house a new business. A plumber and a taxicab operator completed the commercial space.

Above these businesses were the residences and apartments, and behind the building between Madison and Jefferson, a bakeshop. As you can see, we know everybody and could trace relations back several generations, that's how we connect and differentiate who is kin. Many share names but may not be blood-related but named after the slave owner. Another open secret is that many of us have White relations. I know my half-siblings, but none of us would openly acknowledge each other. That is the big paradox about the "Black Code," there is a specific detail about avoiding contact with Black skin, as if one could be contaminated by Blackness, but nobody batted an eye about Black nannies caring for White babies or slave owners having babies with their Black slaves.

Now, let's turn the corner on the right of Strawberry Street at Jefferson, the Colored destination we called Jersey where the whole area would be bustling with activity on weekends and evenings. There were several speakeasies, actually bootleg joints where people, including Whites, would visit secretly for drinks. We could eat at Mary Eliza Wilson Cookshop, famous for Yock and other pork dishes sought after even by White folks.

Greenleaf Beer Garden    Mitchell's Shop

Then on Jefferson, there's Mitchell's Shop which sold tobacco and pop Jessies, those popular pull string cowgirl toys, and squirrel nuts, other penny candies and other neat stuff that kids love. The proprietor was my friend Willis Mitchell, who was the first Colored full-time policeman in Virginia. His daughter Lenora Mitchell was the first Black woman who became a member of the Cape Charles School Board and was one of four who helped integrate the Northampton County Golf Club, which paved the way for all area golf clubs to open their courses to Black players. The building with the payphone outside is historic, as the adjoining Greenleaf Beer Garden on the left which was operated by Mary Mapp and Georgia Jackson, and would be lost if no one rescued them from development into fancy tourist lodgings.

Next door, there was Dale Wilson's Shoeshine stand. Dale was also a member of the Inkspot Quartet. Dale had polio, but he declined to receive any handout or charity and was proud to earn his living. We may catch him and his group warbling often outside of Mitchell's Shop storefront where they'd hang out waiting for their turn at the pay telephone.

On the corner of Peach and Jefferson was a cool place to hang out, and in which, many a time, I was caught by my mother and given a whipping when I was younger: the Little Brown Jug, a restaurant, bar, and dance hall established by Aunt Bea in 1930. I had a drink there once and I couldn't take it, I felt I'd catch on fire if someone lit my breath. The regulars raise a glass before drinking, "Up to it, down to it, God bless the man who ain't up to it," to toast each other. Another popular toast is, "Drink hardy, it's a sad man that's out here rocking somebody else's child when he should be home rocking his own." After that first drink, I didn't try another in this place. Alas, it is a vacant lot now, but some of its sideboards were rescued by the people who built their houses next door as outdoor shower enclosures in the garden courtyard shared by the owners.

Salvaged boards used for outdoor shower

Salvaged board siding from Little Brown Jug

On Plum and Jefferson was T's Corner, formerly Ewell's Grocery, another teen hangout, a restaurant, and grocery operated by Rosetta Treherne. On some days, Frank Williams would park his truck on this corner on his way to the landfill to dump meats that are dated past their freshness to be sold at the supermarket, but still not spoiled and he would distribute it to anyone who wanted it.

On the opposite corner at Jefferson and Plum, is St. Stephen's AME Church. Built in 1885, it was first at 500 Monroe as the Bethany (Northern) Methodist Church and housed the first school in Cape Charles for Whites. In 1889, St. Stephen's purchased it when it became the first school for Blacks, then moved it to its present location in 1912. It is the oldest church building in Cape Charles.

St. Stephen's AME Church

If we continue east on Jefferson to Nectarine then turn right on Madison Avenue, we'all find the First Baptist Church. The building was constructed in 1887 and moved to its present location in 1901. My family had attended this church for a long time since my grandparent's days. The newer Cape Charles Baptist Church on Randolph and Plum built in 1902, is integrated, whereas this First Baptist Church is unintentionally segregated since the remaining congregation is all Black.

The First Baptist Church

Many small mom and pop operations run services from their homes who acquired clientele by word of mouth. One I remember was Miss Zee, a jewel of the neighborhood, the go-to person when special clothing was needed for school or special events. Her sewing area was a small corner in the house she shared with her daughter Jessie Beach and her family. She made tailored clothing for customers all over the county, but she'd put them aside if a student needed her services. She didn't use patterns, she just took your measurement, looked at a photo of the garment, or listened to your description, and she'd just construct the garment and it would be perfect and beautiful.

Sometimes money wasn't available to buy the fabric, so she'd make them from whatever was available, from curtains, men's suits, scraps, and whatnot. Mabel Chapman-Mitchell liked to tell the story of needing crepe paper for a gown to wear for school and she didn't have enough money, so Miss Zee told her to buy the cheaper tissue paper instead and she made a gown that not only was beautiful but endured through the performance.

Quite a few people sold food from their homes to raise money for school or church, or as a weekend income supplement but for many families, they were able to survive by selling these home-cooked foods. You could purchase Yuck from Laura Ayers, hot sausage sandwiches, pig's feet, fried chicken, and barbecue from Janie Washington. On Saturdays, Ruth Bland would set up fried chicken dinners, sandwiches, and cakes, and my mom, Miss Mae, would offer pound cake, hand-cranked ice cream which later became electric. Gladys Henry sold home-made ice cream, melt-in-your-mouth apple pies, marble cakes, and German chocolate cake, said to be often imitated but not duplicated, and Mary Beckett sold home-made rolls. The hosts of weekend card games always sold food to their patrons and the public and were available until the wee hours.

Maria Bivens of Onancock built a successful business from selling her exceptional "one-cent" Aunt Maria's cakes. At her death, the Norfolk Virginian reported she had sold over 3,000,000 cakes and from its proceeds, she had bought her freedom, a valuable farm, and supported her large family.

Businesses big and small catered to every necessary or pleasurable need and there was no reason to patronize the White establishments on Mason Avenue. Davis Taxi Services, Amos Shoes Relais, Mattie Branche's Hair Salon, Cook's Taxi Services, Rosetta Johnson Hair Salon, and Charles Bragg, an expert in the lost art of chair caning, were all owner-operated businesses who made significant contributions to services in the community. If an item was not available locally, then a trip on the ferry across the bay was in order and we could shop in the big department stores in Norfolk or Virginia Beach.

One day I had a whim to go across the Bay with a few of my friends, who were happy to oblige since I was handling all the expenses. I had money on me from my many little businesses and was itching to spend it. We had fun, but I was broke after it was over, and I never repeated the same free-wheeling spending again.

Several doctors also practiced and lived in our neighborhood at various times. Daniel W. Palmer, MD, was born in Henderson, North Carolina, and was the first physician to provide care to the Black community on the Eastern Shore. His office was located at first on Jefferson Avenue then moved it later to Washington Avenue. He worked in a dairy farm to put himself through school, waking up at 4:00 in the morning and working nights running an electric light plant until midnight so he could attend school during the day. With perseverance, he graduated in 1904 from Leonard School of Medicine in North Carolina and moved to Cape Charles in 1910, practicing medicine until 1928. He lived on Peach Street.

William Henderson Johnson, MD I remember well. He was born in Philadelphia and graduated from Meharry Medical School and, with a degree in public health at the University of Pennsylvania, came to practice in Cape Charles from 1929 to 1942. His office was on Mason Avenue. Alice Brinkley Brown worked as his receptionist when she was in high school, as well as Janette Joynes. He returned to Philadelphia to continue his practice and later wrote his memoir, "Memories of an Eastern Shore Physician" in 1988, before he died the following year. He stated that the reason he left Cape Charles was because of his frustration at segregation that prevented him from caring adequately for his patients by the refusal of the hospital to grant him admission privileges. His house on 601 Jefferson Avenue was purchased by Rev Eli and Irene Coles, and later by Diane Davis.

William Sheppard, DDS, was a dentist from Hampton, Virginia. His office was the first floor of his home on Mason Avenue, the same office occupied by Dr. Johnson earlier. He was appreciated because he never turned a patient away no matter what time of day or their ability to pay.

Lottie Sprattley was a midwife who lived on Madison Avenue who had delivered 800 babies successfully and lost only one. She was prevented from further delivering babies when a new gynecologist came to practice and intimidated Lottie about complications she could have delivering babies with her methods. Lottie just stopped practicing after that. She was a very valuable resource to the community who had little access to medical care which was set up mainly for White folks. Black doctors could not continue to care for their patients in the hospital because they were denied admitting privileges. So, a doctor had to refer his patient to a White physician who would treat his Black patient in the hospital hallway since Blacks were not allowed admission to a hospital bed. Even in sickness, you are treated with indignity, which lead many Blacks to forego medical visits until they were in a critical state.

When movies found their way to the Eastern Shore, there were 16 movie theaters in 1931, but there was only one movie theater that allowed Colored folks and only in the balcony: the Stratton at Cheriton, but it burned down in 1940. Washington Tabb, insurance agent, together with William Carey and W. H. Dickinson, formed the Cape Charles Theater Corporation and purchased two lots on 518 and 532 Jefferson Ave, and built the first movie house for Colored folks. Constructed of cinder blocks with 400 seats, the Carver Theater opened on May 24, 1940, and operated until the mid-1950s.

Adjacent to it, the Carver Spot, a soda fountain and restaurant was added in 1947. It was a teen hangout with booths, a jukebox, and a dance floor. Georgia Lyons operated the Spot during our teen years, selling snacks and prepared foods and then the John Waldo, Sr. family took over for a short while after that. The Carver theater was named after the scientist George Washington Carver after a naming contest won by Bessie Trower, my mother's grandaunt. Soon, it became the center of commercial development for local Black businesses. Led by Washington Taub, who was a college graduate and had offices in the theater where he managed both the theater and an insurance agency, he expanded the reach of local businesses by having agents go out of the community to educate his target clients about insurance. Flanked by two churches and several stores, the Carver theater complex became the center of the community, where people came together to eat, shop, worship, and be entertained until it was demolished in the 1980s after serving as the headquarters of The Alpha and Omega Church.

The Jersey Section covering Jefferson Avenue, Madison, Washington, Strawberry Street and Fig

Cape Charles Fishing pier built over the old Government Jetty

Strawberry Street

Grays Funeral Home on Jefferson Avenue

Palace theater

# Chapter 5: Lessons in Black and White

I was working as young as six years old, running errands for my father or accompanying him during his rounds of coordinating construction work with roofers, masons, and bricklayers, White craftsmen needing cement work provided by my father.

One day, I was waiting for my father as he discussed his work with the roofer and an older gentleman who was sitting there in the shop signaled me to come near him. He roughly touched my hair without asking and began picking at my roots as if looking for something. Suddenly, he pulled it and announced triumphantly for everyone to hear, "You've got a bug here!" He laughed and flicked the tuft of hair at me. I had a full head of hair as a boy, tightly curled and massed on my scalp. It hurt when he pulled my hair out and I didn't like it, but all I could do was move away, feeling upset.

Many years later, I realized I felt humiliated and helpless, as the gesture was an insult. Publicly, I was being shamed as an unkempt and unwashed child who was harboring louse in my hair. In reality, Black hair, because of its texture, does not harbor lice as much as White hair does. In school, whenever lice were discovered in your hair, the kids made fun of you and called you names and avoided you because you were contagious and dirty. Then you knew you'd stink some more because you'd have to wash your hair with this horrible medicine until the pests were eradicated.

The man was doing the same thing to me, shaming me as if I had the lice, but I knew I couldn't protest. This happened every time I stepped into this shop. Mr. Taylor, the roofer, would be inside talking with my father and did not know this was going on in his shop. I didn't know whether I was told not to say anything, or I just picked up this passive response from observing behaviors around me.

Every day, I was subjected to indignities similar to this, and I learned to accept it as normal. When we traveled on the train, I would automatically sit in the back where the Colored sat, same with the bus, and in the waiting area on the ferry, there were signs assigning where the Colored sat to wait and where Whites sat.

If we were driving to Onancock or Pocomoke, my mother would pack chicken and drinks because we could not buy from stores along the road, and the speed that those cars were driven was no more than 45 miles an hour, so it took a long time to reach our destination. There were no toilet facilities for Blacks so we would get out of the car and relieve ourselves in the woods or just stand and put our backs to the road. I'd even see men and women relieve themselves behind the grocery shop.

When I came in to purchase at a store, I had to give way to a White customer at the cashier counter, even if I was ahead in the queue. In restaurants, we could purchase food but we couldn't eat it at the tables inside, even if we worked as waiters and cooks in the same restaurant. Black women cleaned the hotels in town and did the laundry and changed the bedsheets, but they couldn't book a room for their family to stay. However, Whites could book a bed in my mother's house and would be received with the same hospitality and respect as any customer, Colored or White.

I knew about this man who had escorted the mail from Philadelphia and the train would arrive at night, so he had to sleep overnight. There were hotels right across the train depot but he couldn't go there, so he had to walk further to book a bed in my mother's inn. In the morning when I went to deliver the papers, I observed women I knew from church silently make their way to clean the railcars inside and out, then the station waiting area and the ferry all day, hardly pausing to rest. Other women would go to private homes and clean and wash and take care of White people's homes and their children from sunrise to sundown then go home and repeat the same in their own homes.

Everyone worked hard, took pride in their work, and guaranteed its high quality. People's businesses thrived by their reputation. Yet, Whites who hired Black workers insulted them by setting traps to see if they were honest. For example, rigging up carpets and sofas with devices, so that they could tell if the cleaning woman swept underneath, or deliberately leaving money in the open to test if the cleaning women would steal it.

I was exposed to this growing up and I, too, learned to hustle early as I ran my entrepreneurial business from the age of six years old. At first, I ran errands for my father. Then, I got to know the businesspeople and I cut their grass in the summer, delivered orders and got the newspaper delivery service exclusively. I was well-known around as my daddy's son and felt privileged by this position.

Ironically, this did not spare me the daily humiliations and belittling meted out to Blacks who were treated as second class citizens by the White community. And while you were belittled, you were also limited in your achievement or hindered in your success by underhanded obstacles thrown your way. Things such as harassment by changing policies or qualifying requirements; by repeated demands for documentations not required from White candidates; or un-helpfulness by withholding information, not trusting your recommendation or diagnosis of a problem until a White worker could confirm it, often at great inconvenience.

The response to these daily and ever-present indignities came together in an incident when I was around ten years old that I would never forget, and perhaps shaped my actions as an adult.

My mother went into a confectionery store and was about to pay for her purchase at the cashier counter when I stepped into the store to check on her. As soon as I entered, a White customer got a hold of me and slapped me hard across my ears which almost sent me off my feet.

He commanded forcefully, "Get out of here, boy!"

The old confectionery store,
now Brown Dog

From the corner of my eye, I saw my mother fly to my side, enraged. Without hesitation, she looked the man in the eyes, and in a clear, measured voice told him, "Sir, I'd soon see myself drown in my own blood if you lay your hand again on this boy!"

As my mother dragged me out of that store, everyone stood stunned, speechless, and immobilized. What she did was so bold because it violated the unspoken rule that no Black should ever look at a White man directly in the eyes, they should always hold their heads down when speaking to a White man. It gave me the courage to act what I felt after seeing my mother's brave defense of me and helped me manage my fear of the White establishment. I became aware of the difference in the lives of Whites and Blacks and, thinking about my parents as an example, I wanted to help in erasing this difference.

# Chapter 6: How to be Black

I went to the segregated Cape Charles Elementary School from 1945 to 1952. It was a Rosenwald School, which opened for Black children in grades 1-7 in 1929 and was built on 2.5 acres of land purchased from the railroad outside of the main town district. next to the city dump.

Back then I thought, "Why did they build our school next to the dump where the city threw their garbage, all the gutted remains from fish processing, and all manner of refuse?" But I did not dwell on it and soon I accepted it as normal. I was just happy to have a school of our own and to be able to act like ourselves instead of thinking about all the rules pounded into us by our parents to act carefully with Whites.

My mother was adamant that I did not go into White stores to buy anything without an adult present. I was also taught to not speak unless spoken to, and if I did, I should look down and remember to answer respectfully with "Yes-sirs" and "Yes- ma'ams," and never ever look any White man directly in the face. I must avert my face sideways and look down so I would not accidentally look the White man in his eyes.

Also, I must not touch the White man. If I was paying him, I must put my money on the counter and let him take it. I should wait for him to put my change down on the counter and pick it up from the counter, so I do not touch him. I could not use the same cup or drink from the same water fountain if a White man had used it. I could go on and on, about this not touching or mixing with the White man. And even though my mother made sure that we were clean and scrubbed thoroughly, I began to be self-conscious about myself being filthy. I began to be so meticulous about my appearance and how I dressed, that looking back, my peers perhaps saw me as being uppity.

The attention about cleanliness in myself made me note as a child, the concern I had about our neighbor when I discovered that they did not have indoor plumbing and had to bathe in the public marble showers located at Randolph and Strawberry, in the old customs house located inside the post office, before going to school. I couldn't define this issue then, but now I understood that segregation attacked our basic sense of pride and dignity by treating our Blackness as being permanently dirty and, therefore deserving of being shunned and ashamed.

I didn't understand why I was bullied by my Colored peers when all I wanted was to be one of them. I reasoned it must be because I didn't hang out with them after school, but I didn't have time because I was working. Perhaps it was because I was working and had my own money. I realized my family circumstance was more privileged compared to most of them. We had a telephone, electricity and several vehicles because of my father's business.

I was walking home alone from school and these two brothers began heckling me from their porch, for no reason at all except that I was passing by their house on the corner of Monroe Avenue and Fig Street. I didn't know what possessed me then, but in a flash, I charged the two on their porch and chased them inside as they retreated to their mother's protection. Our fistfight was broken up without any physical evidence of it like cuts or bruises on me, and teir mother sent me home without telling my parents, which spared me the rod from my mother who would've surely punished me for what I did. I had many more fistfights in school, but the key was to keep it from my mother, and all would be well. Besides, in these fistfights, I was merely defending myself from the bullies who picked on me. I was not about to complain to my mother and solicit her protection.

I had been driving a car without a license since I was twelve and got paid to do it. Miss Alice Brinkley was a teacher who lived on Jefferson

Avenue. She bought a car, a green 1950 Pontiac before she knew how to drive, so she paid me to drive her wherever she needed to go and subsequently to teach her to drive. I was little then and I remember I had to use the side mirror when backing up since I could not reach to see the rear-view mirror. But I had the most fun driving my father's dumpster truck and operating its shift gears to lift the dump truck bed up and down.

Since many of the business owners knew my father, they accepted that my daddy needed me to help. They didn't object and looked the other way. In time, I knew all the business owners and they knew me. When riding the ferry, they'd give me a generous portion or extra meat whenever I'd buy lunch without charging me extra, and the vendor who I knew would hand it to me almost triumphantly like it was empowering to defy the White owner's authority by having this clandestine transaction under his nose. I would simultaneously feel a thrill like a co-conspirator in an act of defiance of an authority. It seemed an indirect way to get back, to fight, and to assert ourselves so that we didn't feel as helpless.

I observed many situations like this. Blacks could not receive payment; the cashier was always a White man regardless of whether he could read or calculate, and someone I knew regularly stole money from the payments and the cashier couldn't tell whether the change was correct or not.

I would have this same thrill, a sense of triumph mixed with fear of discovery and punishment, every time I found myself in similar situations. We walked to school six blocks from my house on Jefferson Avenue, on the bridge over the railroad track we named "the Hump," down the steps on one side of the overpass where Rayfield's is now. Many times we took the street through the woods, cut across the field to the farms, and in the summer when the watermelon was ripe, we'd help ourselves to some.

We didn't need any tool to open them, and you didn't have to be a surgeon either. Wer'd take a nice one and drop it on a stone to break it and then scramble to be first to grab the cool red spongy and juicy heart of the fruit, the sweetest taste when our throats were parched by the sun. We were a good team and we were fast. We'd eat it on the fly and be at school on time. And although it would be a serious thing if we got caught, for nobody could sit down for a bit after that, I believe it was the quest for this sense of power that I desired to be accepted by the bullies in school. I admired their easy manner of resisting conformist behavior and acting as they please without fear.

The watermelon farm beyond
the railroad track

I remember that the one source of pride amongst us boys was to have our own buck knife. We'd play games with it during our recess, have carving games with it, and whatnot. We also played root the pig, which was definitely a no-no, and shoot marbles. The girls would play double Dutch and marble jacks.

Our school had central heat and I knew the custodian. He'd let me and some of the boys have the key to release the steam from the radiator which was so much fun we fought over who should do it. One time, I was late, and we sneaked into our classroom through a window. Our teacher caught me and, of course, my mother was told about it. I got whipped at school by the teacher and one more time at home by my mother.

Our teachers then were strict with us because they wanted us to learn. Education was emphasized and we were glad we could go to school. Our parents and teachers worked together to give us the best education. We were made to understand that we should go as far as we could in learning, even better than our parents, so we could have better jobs and improve our lot. Nobody gave it a second thought that we were segregated. In fact, we liked it better that way because we could all be ourselves and did not have to act afraid because we might do the wrong thing like how it was with White people.

We had our own school events and competitions. We had softball and baseball games and sometimes, when we couldn't go to certain places like the museums or theater, our teacher would show us pictures of paintings and sculptures so we would know how these things looked, so we would be prepared for high school.

The whole community participated in our education. There were several persons in the town who went to college. We knew a gentleman who worked as a longshoreman and a musician and he let us go to his house on Sundays and listen to classical music. He had all sorts of musical instruments that we could learn to play if we were interested: violin, viola, cello. We put up plays, sang in a choir, and had school dances.

We looked forward to these dances. We'd push all the desks to one side since we didn't have a gym and had our school dance. It was very nice. Our parents would chaperone, and they also had fun. It was so much fun that my parents let us have these dances in our garage. We'd decorate it and have sock hops that all the young people in our community could attend.

We also didn't have a cafeteria, so some parents would come in and fix us lunch and after lunch, we'd go out and play. Our teacher would eat her lunch at her desk, but we could go to her if we needed help.

The most fun day was the May Day Festival. We'd dress up in White shirts and the girls would dress up in multicolored dresses and have matching ribbons around a pole and dance around it. There would be a May Day King and Queen who presided over the events. Alas, we lost this tradition after integration. Perhaps there will be enough interest to revive this, as a historical event.

We were aware we didn't have everything that the White school had. In fact, we only had their hand-me-down books and the pictures all had White faces. I remember images of little girls with yellow hair and their parents with the family dog smiling and looking happy. I couldn't see myself in it, but we just accepted it as normal. We didn't mind because we got the books and learned the words anyway. We didn't know what the White school had, but our teachers were the best. We took learning seriously because everybody worked seriously to teach us. I may have goofed off a few times and may have had many fistfights at school while I was with the gang, but my mother soon put a stop to all of that and I buckled down to study and graduated in 1952.

It was a big deal to graduate from Cape Charles Elementary. We prepared for seven years to get to that point. The importance of this graduation could be gleaned from how seriously we took this event by dressing up in our better-than-Sunday outfits and the girls, especially, would look very pretty in their dresses. We had graduation capes and togas and marched down the room. As the principal called our names, we walked across the stage to receive our diploma, that little paper that told us we could transfer to Northampton County Public High School, from the Colored school over "the Hump."

The "Hump", Railroad Overpass to Old Cape Charles Road

Cape Charles Colored School

Historic Marker

# Chapter 7: A Rude Awakening

I was aware of segregation before going to high school, but unless I was in the town on an errand for my father or mother, at the Savage Drug Store where I couldn't sit down at the soda fountain, or couldn't go to the beach except to the little section at the end of Washington Avenue where the ferries used to come in, I didn't experience it on an unrelenting basis.

After graduation from Cape Charles Elementary, I went to high school starting in the 8th grade at the segregated Northampton County Public High School in Machipongo. The Cape Charles High School on Peach Street was the White school from Grades 1-12. Virginia resisted integration of schools after the Brown vs. Board of Education ruling in 1958, with the Virginia Assembly issuing its Southern Manifesto.

Schools remained physically segregated. In 1960, the county school system consolidated the high schools at Cape Charles and Machipongo into the Northampton High School in Eastville. It admitted White and Black students, but classes remained physically segregated within the school. Students were classified into the academic or general group and the practical or slow group. And guess which group the Colored were assigned to?

We were made to feel we were not wanted; the teachers were not the same as in the Colored school and some were downright nasty, and although we didn't have much trouble with the kids, their parents were open in their disapproval of our presence. Whereas before, I didn't give segregation much thought and accepted it as normal, here I began to see the inequality and questioned why.

While in college in the early '60s, I was carried by the tide of the Civil Rights Movement sweeping the nation. The feeling of being a second-class citizen and being marginalized intensified after I entered the workplace and began to experience the direct impact of unequal treatment. The experience of trying to get licensed as an electrician still rankles me to this day.

I had acquired considerable skill as an electrician by observing, self-study, and doing actual work for friends and relatives and thought I'd apply for a license and become a professional and charge fees accordingly. One requirement was to have your work inspected by the county. I had difficulty scheduling my inspections on a timely basis because the inspector was located at a distant office. This went on for a long time until I learned from an outside source that there was a local inspector who had plenty of time available. The local county office that was supposed to give this information never bothered to give me this information, knowing full well that I had repeatedly tried to schedule an inspection with them.

The next obstacle I had to hurdle was in the application for a license. The requirements I had to satisfy exceeded the requirements for a White applicant, who could obtain a license readily based on practical on-the-job training as demonstrated by many successful job inspections, which I already had fulfilled. But I was required to complete an expensive full semester course in a vocational training school. I was incensed by the blatant unfairness and the smug attitudes of the White county employees, but I had to give in to the injustice because I had no power to protest. The White establishment had locked in their control by having their relatives appointed to government jobs, the judges and jury were all White, with attitudes still encoded in the Black Code laws passed since the Revolution and given fresh expression in the Jim Crow era of segregation, that Whites were the superior race and Blacks were inherently inferior and destined to be ruled by the White man as he sees fit. And what the White man did was to pass laws that put up obstacles for the Black man in order for him to compete fairly for skilled jobs, equal wages, education, housing, and access to protections and opportunity. Such laws were intended to keep the Black man from rising, by holding him down to service and labor jobs.

And today, the Black man is still trying to prove that he is an equal human being to any White man, still enduring the indignities and dehumanizing treatment.

I was sheltered from this reality during much of the era of segregation because of my family's protectiveness by keeping me within the enclave of our homogeneous Black society and by my relatively privileged upbringing brought about by my parents' social standing in our community. I did not fully appreciate that their status in our community was obtained at great sacrifice through their hard work and endurance of daily indignities. But the world is bigger than this sheltered world I grew up in and I realized then that I had a family and children to worry about now. I didn't want them to grow up in a world where they were made to believe in the lies about our inherent nature: that being Black is inferior to being White.

So, I set out to prove that I could be a skilled electrician and could earn as much as any White man by obtaining my electrician license. I enrolled in vocational school, obtained my electrician certificate, and dared to compete with the White electricians for jobs. I gave it up after finding that the job involved physical agility such as climbing or wiggling into small spaces, which didn't appeal much to me, but not before I'd proven that a Black man could do an equal, if not a better, job at it.

# Chapter 8: A Gathering Place

Something was always going on at my parent's place of business, Gray's Funeral Home. The funeral home occupied three city lots of property between Madison and Jefferson Avenue. We reached it by the alleys running from Nectarine Street to Washington Avenue, and we'd come to a compound with three buildings, our house on 625 Madison Ave, the garage and the storage shed where my father stored the bulk supply of concrete, and the Gray's Funeral Home on 618 Jefferson Avenue. It was the hub for social events and meetings and people needing help invariably found their way there.

I remember hoboes regularly dropped in, those men who hitched a free ride on freight trains to wherever they were going. Others called them tramps, but my mother always welcomed them with a hot meal, and sometimes they'd stay for the night and my mother would let them sleep in the shed or the yard in warm weather. I got to know a few of them, but I never learned why they liked to move from place to place without saying goodbye or telling their families.

Over the years, some of their kin would be looking for them in our house or another hobo would come, and they'd let us know that someone had passed. They didn't like to tell their stories; I was told that some may be hiding from the law. I remember a few of them, they were a diverse group, and not all were tramps. A soldier was one of them. Another went to college, a professional man. I wondered why he rode the trains without any particular destination. I think he told me that he just wanted to be alone, but I still didn't understand why. A few worked for my father's concrete business, earning just enough for their next trip. One stayed for a year and was a good worker. My mother let him sleep in the shed or the garage, and I'd see him wash in the outdoor faucet by the shed and use the outhouse. Then one day, he just left without saying goodbye. In a way, through word of mouth among the hoboes, our place was identified as a refuge where they could rest and have a hot meal.

My mother did this without any financial help in the beginning. Later, the churches pitched in and organized social services to the Black Community were provided through charity groups like Eastern Star, Masons, and House of Ruth. The County government only had a poorly funded token program consisting of a single White social worker, who implemented the government qualifying policy at her whim and only approved aid to those she favored. The Black clientele thought she was mean as a junkyard dog. Applicants opted not to receive any services rather than be subjected to the humiliation of getting help from her. You couldn't complain to anyone because most of the government employees were her kin.

You could reach the funeral home without being seen from the street. This was especially important during the Jim Crow era when my parents held meetings to strategize in order to have basic services such as streetlights, sewer and water, and street paving provided by the City and County governments, and later during the Civil Rights era to plan sit-ins and protests. There were discussions about how to change things and there were secret meetings at home where important people met.

I remember the fear in everyone because of the law of 1806. I looked up this law later and found out that these were a series of laws passed by the Virginia General Assembly in response to the threat perceived by the White establishment of increasing numbers of Freedmen who were emancipated after the Revolution. It severely restricted the freedom of both slaves and Freedmen by prohibiting assembly and travel. Its confined Blacks to the plantations and, if caught outside without papers or permission from the master, they would face punishment by the whip or in the case of a Freedman, re-enslavement. Slave patrols roamed the countryside to enforce the law, ruthlessly hunting down their quarry with hounds. Once apprehended the runaway slaves were subjected to extreme punishment, including lynching. The terror this situation created was incomprehensible now. I didn't understand the need for secrecy in meetings and the need for subterfuge until I realized that. I began high school and questioned the inequality of life under segregation.

As a gathering place for fun, we had sock hops at the garage with dancing and music all night. We also met there after school where we played basketball. My father had the space over the garage as his private man cave where he'd have his friends over for drinks.

Neighbors would come to use our telephone as we were one of the first 38 in Cape Charles and the only one on our street to have a telephone and I couldn't help overhearing their business during their call. I believe I was a loner by nature, but I was observant and curious and there was plenty to hear, see, and do in our backyard. The excitement came to me rather than me going out to seek it.

Later, at the end of active Civil Rights protests with the passage of the Civil Rights Act of 1964, the funeral home became the meeting place to launch political campaigns to elect Black candidates. I honed my skills and gained experience from these associations and was the first African-American to be elected to the Cape Charles City Council and the Northampton Board of Supervisors for three terms as well as serving one term as Chairman.

Old Family home on Madison Avenue

The Storage shed, renovation interrupted by Covid-19 pandemic

The alley

The Compound

The funeral home on Jefferson Ave

The Garage, renovation interrupted by Covid-19 pandemic

Our Home on Monroe Avenue

# Chapter 9: Sit-Ins and Protests

After the Civil War, the United States had an increasing population of Blacks who had served in the Union Army and were returning as free men, who were allowed to keep the guns that were issued during their military service. Meanwhile, the White soldiers returning who fought with the former Confederate States were stripped of their weapons and were required to make an oath of loyalty to the United States before they were granted amnesty. In the three years after the war, the Eastern Shore witnessed flareups of racial violence that targeted the Freedmen. The White establishment became alarmed about the large numbers of former enslaved Blacks and couldn't abide by the possibility that Blacks, who were exercising their voting rights then, could be ruling them. A series of laws were passed by the Virginia Legislature which codified the lies that were the foundation of racism in the Black Code laws that defined slavery and had been implemented by the Confederate States before the Civil War. They were created with the intent to restore White supremacy by disenfranchisement and remove the freedom and civil protections achieved by Blacks during the Reconstruction.

In my younger years, I took it that the way I lived my life was normal since everyone took the rules for Black behavior as a given without question, and to protest would be futile since nothing could be done about it. I endured the indignity and insults and the helplessness until I saw more intimately how Whites lived. In my daily rounds delivering the paper into White homes, I saw them in lesser esteemed circumstances.

I knew and accepted as normal that Blacks could not go through the front door of White folks' homes but must use the back or kitchen entrance, but some would give me special instructions about depositing the paper inside the door or some would ask me inside to hand them their paper while they were having breakfast. I got to see the interior of the White homes and what kind of furnishings they had. In many homes, I found the furniture to be cheaper and of poorer quality than what my parents and neighbors had whose homes were furnished with expensive antiques and fine quality furnishings. In judging their clothes, the tailoring was not as fine as what our Black tailors would create. And our women's clothes were more fashionable and better made, and Black women certainly had more dresses to wear for any occasion.

I began to see that if Blacks could have just as much and better material possessions than the White folks, then they were just as good and capable of doing whatever they wished as any White folk. I also observed that the wives of White men had less freedom in expressing their thoughts and were also bound by stringent behavior rules to follow, very similar to behavior rules for Blacks. They were unable to make simple decisions like how they wanted me to deliver their paper or how they wanted their grass cut and would refer me to their husbands for answers. Speaking with a Black man was a strong taboo that they observed.

In contrast, in my family, I only knew women who were confident, strong, industrious, self-sufficient, well-educated, engaged in the community, and courageous, like my mother, grandmother, my wife, and aunts. These early observations broke the certitude for me of the belief that held the superiority of the White race over Black.

In my sophomore year of college, while I was attending Virginia Union University, there were many sit-in protests going on to force the desegregation of eating establishments in Richmond. I participated in a sit-in at one of the restaurants on Lombardy Street, the White Tower. I went inside the dining room and sat at a table with three other protesters and asked to be served. Ordinarily, the establishment would order us to leave or call the police and have us arrested if we refused to move. We were hoping to be arrested, for the police to throw us in jail, but instead, the establishment just ignored us, didn't serve us but let us remain there sitting until we decided to leave after thirty or forty-five minutes of the sit-in. That first sit-in was a disappointment, but I found out that we did not do it properly, that we had to remain seated until we were served or arrested.

On another occasion, I was going to participate in a protest organized in Petersburg, seventeen miles from Richmond at Virginia State University where Juanita, my girlfriend then was enrolled, but I couldn't get transportation right away and after hitchhiking on a truck, I arrived at the city center to find it weirdly quiet as a church mouse. In those days, we either walked or hitchhiked to wherever we were going, and on campus, there were no buses. In Cape Charles, I could get a ride easily by going to the truck farm just outside of the city. I got to know many of the truck drivers and their routes and could pick a ride with the most likely driver to match my schedule, but not this time. I arrived too late and the protest crowd had dispersed.

That was another damper to my enthusiasm. Anyway, I was considered by the student protest leaders to not have the temperament to engage in this passive non-violent approach, that I was too impatient and too sensitive to be subjected to indignities and that I could be pushed to my limit easily and could be impulsive in my action. That ended my organized sit-in protest in college, but not my efforts in effecting desegregation.

One auspicious day I was about to leave the cafeteria until I suddenly recognized the Reverend Martin Luther King, Jr. by the door. I was so close to him that I could shake his hand and talk to him but then he was gone before I could mobilize myself to act. Seeing him in the flesh, I felt the pride and awe of being in his presence and I was inspired by his energy and passion to do my share of realizing his dream for social justice and freedom. This led me to going to a movie at the Palace which, after word of my impulsive action got around, ended the practice of rejecting entrance to Blacks, even if once inside, we were still shunned by social distancing

The effort it took to integrate the Northampton County Golf and Country Club became the ultimate challenge that tested my determination to break down the color barrier. The golf course was just in my backyard at the end of Monroe Avenue, where the Bay creek Resort Development begins at Bahama Road today, but I couldn't't play it. I had to tee off all the way in Pocomoke at a 9-hole course and play it twice for a complete round.

So, I organized a group to apply for membership, prepared to use litigation if our application was rejected and engaged Denise Bland, a lawyer with an office on Randolph Avenue for that purpose. The applicants I recruited were leaders and pillars of the Black community whose credentials, if they had been White, were a shoo-in for admission. William S. Smith was the Assistant Superintendent of the Northampton County Schools, Thomas Stratton was a member of the Cape Charles City Council, Lenora Mitchell was a Board Member of the Cape Charles School, and I was Chairman of the Northampton County Board of Supervisors. Two members were required to sponsor an applicant, and at first, our application languished without sponsorship until we found support in Robert Thomas and Charlie Powell. I am grateful to these two gentlemen who braved being shunned by their White peers and risked losing their jobs by acting contrary to the rules of White behavior towards Blacks.

Many of the 250 members of the club didn't attend meetings when our application was on the agenda for voting, and when it was presented only about fifteen members were present and who rejected our application at least seven times over the three to four years that it took before I talked with Harry Alston, the Vice President of Brown and Root, the energy company who owned the golf club.

At the time, Brown and Root was negotiating with Northampton County and Cape Charles Governing Boards for the annexation of the resort project they were developing on the remainder of the land purchase made by William S. Scott to build the railroad town of Cape Charles. Harry, it appeared, had forgotten his company's ownership of the club and was unaware of our pending application when I pointed out to him the irony of his seeking our approval for annexation when we could not even play in the golf course that his company-owned.

After hearing this, he met with the golf course administration and told them to admit me and my group or he would close the golf course. In three days, our membership was approved. Harry Alston as representative of Brown and Root could do this because his company had more wealth than any of the local elites and therefore could wield power over them. But, as I was driving through Chicago, Michigan, and Ohio on vacation with my family I didn't get the news right away. I didn't know about it until my group caught up with me, calling to let me know. My fellow golfers decided to play without me, excited to test their member privilege before I could return to stage a grand tee off spectacle for the White golfers who opposed our inclusion. We played every Wednesday, and after I brought White and Black people of importance as my guests, such as the Governor, those unhappy with our membership relented in their objection and adopted a more welcoming attitude.

After word got around that I was a member of this golf club, I was able to get tee times to other golf clubs in the area, and after me, Blacks were able to gain access to these White establishments as well. We had to discharge Denise Bland, the attorney we engaged for litigation, as we didn't need to go to court after all.

# Chapter 10: Race Politics

The Boy Scouts organization was a very important component of a young boy's life in those days. My son wanted to join the boy scouts but there was only one group for White children. However, because people knew me, my children were admitted until a new den mother who didn't know me ran the group and kicked my children out. I was forced to organize a Boy Scout and a Boy's Club so that my children and any child could participate, but by default, it became a segregated group as no White children applied to be admitted. Integration gradually happened after the two groups would combine for camping trips or events organized by the military.

The military helped in facilitating change since it became indefensible to expect Blacks to fight to preserve freedom for others when they, themselves, do not have it at home. Black enlisted men had expectations of equality in the service extended outside of military bases. I found myself in the role of initiating these changes as I encountered them in raising my family.

I became instrumental in reviving Masonry by reorganizing and recruiting new members, in opening the membership to the Northampton County Golf Club to Blacks, and admittance into the Palace Theater.

In Cape Charles, I became aware of problems that needed to be addressed politically by listening to the people who gathered at the funeral home to discuss issues that needed changing. There was an awareness of the absence of Black participation in the process due to lack of education about responsible citizenship, inexperience in community organizing, and White intimidation and laws intended to suppress the Black vote.

I came of age in politics just as the nation was also moving towards change and I benefited from the educational and training opportunities offered through the Joint Center for Political Studies supported by the Ford Foundation at Howard University, to help Blacks gain a foothold in the mainstream political process. It provided technical assistance to Black elected officials as many are new at their jobs and needed to learn the ropes in day to day administration and political networking, and couldn't count on the help of their more experienced and better connected White colleagues, as many still held the bias of White supremacy and were loath to see Blacks take political control after the Civil Rights movement. Black politicians had no seniority as they were prevented from the electoral process by laws enacted after Reconstruction until the Civil Rights Movement provided the legal access.

The Black community had not experienced full citizenship with voting rights but for a mere half-century. In Virginia, Black politicians had been unable to form Black Caucuses for a decade due to entrenched racial attitudes and fewer elected Black officials, hence there was no support for local officials from the organized national Black Caucuses. Before Virginia had the resources to organize its Black Caucus where I was a charter member, I participated in training workshops where I learned about community organizing and voter registration and how government works. When I decided to run for a seat in the Cape Charles City Council, I applied this knowledge in organizing door-to-door voter registration and urged everyone to vote for me and educated my recruits about how change could occur in the political arena.

It is not surprising to me that for many years no other Black candidate made it to the Virginia State Legislature after Peter Jacob Carter. He was a slave in Eastvale who ran away in 1863 when he was eighteen and joined the Union Army's Company B of the 10th Regiment USCT. He became the first African-American elected to the Virginia

Legislature as a Republican representing Northampton County in 1871, the year after the 15th amendment was ratified into the constitution. He held that position until 1878 by winning his election three more times. After his election, a series of laws had been enacted that systematically disenfranchised the Black voter, and it is still going on today even after the election of Barack Obama, the first Black POTUS. In 1879 Peter Carter lost his bid for the Virginia Senate after conservatives gerrymandered him out of the district and due to his support of aggressively repaying Virginia's antebellum debts, he lost the votes of Blacks who were living in poverty after emancipation.

After his loss however, he remained a prominent Black leader on the Eastern Shore. When he died in 1886, he was only forty-one years old. His last-born son from his second marriage to Maggie Treherne, William Carter, changed his name to Peter Carter, after his father's death and became a doctor and headed the Surgery Department of the Veteran's Hospital at Tuskegee, Alabama.

Peter Jacob Carter had been many things during his lifetime, a slave, a soldier, a politician, a college rector, a landowner, a farmer, a justice of the peace, a lighthouse keeper, a husband, a father, but he remains the only Black person from the Eastern Shore who was elected to the Virginia legislature.

Representative William P. Robinson, Sr., was Norfolk's first Black legislator since the Reconstruction. He was elected to the Virginia Assembly and served for six terms from 1970 to 1980. I admired him and sought him out as a mentor. He taught me the "one-shot vote" strategy.

When I announced my candidacy for the Cape Charles City Council, I ignored the advice of the church elders who have counseled past unsuccessful candidates not to bother with the Jersey residents, for traditionally they have not voted or expressed any interest in change. I recognized this elitism among us by appealing to this segment of the population in Cape Charles. I knew many of them and identified that they were just too intimidated by the voter registration process designed to discourage them. There is a danger of police arrest if they congregate in numbers at meetings and registration is processed by White folks in a White-owned location whose attitudes were not welcoming, if not outright intimidating and many could not afford the $1.50 poll tax that is required to get on the voter rolls.

Through door-to-door efforts, I persuaded seventy-five of them to register, and by not ignoring the power of their votes and combining it with the strategy of the "one-shot vote" I broke the losing streak of past unsuccessful campaigns. The strategy involved asking voters to vote only for one candidate, choosing me whenever there is a choice of voting for several candidates, which was the case for the City Council seat. By not diluting the vote to other candidates I won a landslide victory; the first Black to be elected to the Cape Charles City Council.

The strategy worked for two more terms and later for my subsequent election as a member of the Northampton County Board of Supervisors for three terms with the appointment as Chairman of the Board on my last term. I became the to-go person when the community needed Black representation in various agencies and although I became the token Black appointed to these various boards, it didn't matter, I tried to do what I could to improve our presence and representation by naming the first Black woman to the Housing and Redevelopment Board of Northampton and Accomack County when I was its Chairman and helped elect Alice Brinkley Brown, the first Black female Mayor of Cape Charles.

Others came forth to be important in obtaining recognition for the progress in our community, such as Lenora Mitchell, who was the first Black woman to serve on the Cape Charles School Board and Odelle Collins, who was appointed to a seat at the Chesapeake Bay Bridge-Tunnel Commission Board. She lived on Jefferson Avenue, attended the school at "the Hump," and kept our high school alumni together by organizing the reunion of the Northampton County High School graduates every two years for thirty years whose numbers reach over 2000 now. She was educated as a teacher and was an indefatigable fundraiser for various projects benefiting the community. I became Secretary and Chairman of the Selective Service Board and had a series of Gubernatorial Appointments to the Virginia Beach Board under Governor Gerald Baliles, Linwood Holton, and Douglas Wilder, and served VA Representative Robert Bloxom, at his pleasure.

As the first African-American to be elected a member of the Cape Charles Town Council and the Northampton Board of Supervisors, I was the only Black member, and I felt frustrated by the difficulty of getting attention and action to the issues I bring. I worked on a tourism proposal to revitalize the town after its decline, obtained a grant to submit a development plan and took trips to observe cities undergoing redevelopment, but my proposal didn't get any support and the plan languished until something very similar was proposed by my White colleagues and then it got acted upon.

I was young and inexperienced but the biggest challenge I had to overcome was to be listened to, as I had to push back against centuries of White disregard of the Black man, of his treating the Black man as ignorant and being dismissive of any ideas that are contributed by the Black man. I learned to mobilize support from my constituents by organizing attendance and training my community on how to present their issues to the board. These public service activities kept me overextended at times, but felt I needed to do them as my contribution to realize the dream of racial equality. My efforts brought much satisfaction when I could achieve my goal, but as the work involved is time-consuming and misunderstood when a positive outcome is not achieved, I felt increasingly frustrated and disheartened about ever achieving true social equality. It takes a toll to maintain grace and humor when one has to, to this day, deal daily with White prejudice where you are discounted as ignorant and ignored by dismissive behavior and sabotaged in your efforts by trickery or malice if it appears that you are getting ahead of the White man.

Also, the work of engaging the Black community in continuing citizen involvement in the governing and political process is not sustainable without strong leadership, as the participation remains still on a personal level that is limited to family issues and does not translate into individual behavior directed at general progress. But the most regressive of all to progress is having to deal with the Black Code, the ongoing legacy of slavery that imprisons many Blacks in feeling betrayed when one of them does not behave within their boundaries, for not knowing how to stay in one's place was once a cause of extreme disruption in a slave's well-being, leading to the withdrawal of approval and privileges, severe punishment, separation from loved ones, or death. As someone who did not behave according to my place, at times perceived as an Uncle Tom, I felt alone in my work and misunderstood by my own people.

The Bay Creek Property across Monroe and Fulcher where the Northampton County Golf and Country Club used to be

The Baycreek property next to Monroe Ave, where the 2nd hole of the golf course used to be just outside my front yard.

Listening to Senator Paul Tribble

# Chapter 11: The Church and Community

The church and my faith in the goodness of God have helped me to remain calm during so many adverse times. Religion has been a guiding force for my family and a source of comfort. It helps me to understand my past, provides insight into the present, and gives me hope for the future. I am grateful that it has always been part of my family's history.

My paternal grandfather, Jacob Godwin, was at church one Sunday at the African Baptist Church in Cheriton when he noticed my grandmother Candis and introduced himself to her. I grew up attending the First Baptist Church on Nectarine and Madison with my parents and continued for a long time. I continued to be an active member of the congregation with my family after they passed and served as a trustee later. However, my religious experience was influenced by my maternal grandparents from a very early age, my grandfather and grandmother Joynes.

Prayer was central in their daily practice. As soon as they were out of bed, they were on their knees praying. Before breakfast, they prayed to give them a good start for the day. They were kneeling in prayer to start every meal and after their day's work, again they had prayers and scripture. Their day began and ended in prayer, giving thanks to the Lord for answering their supplication for a good harvest by guiding them in the timing of crop rotation, in planting and reaping, for their good health, for realizing favors from others as well as providing favors to others. They lived a life of prayer and service to others and the community as Christ-like servants and they prayed for the entire family and prayed with us to be faithful to the family and others.

I was a witness to their abounding faith in the Holy Trinity: our father, God, his son, Jesus Christ, and the Holy Spirit that guides, comforts, sustains, and fills the conviction of believers. The Holy Spirit is central in this belief and is mentioned more than thirty times in the Book of Acts of the Holy Bible. My maternal grandparents had an ear for God, they knew His voice and took heed. They made no major decisions without consulting God. They taught us that to disobey His voice resulted in failure, whereas obedience resulted in acts of kindness, referred to as "blessing."

Sunday was a day of reverence. We were required by our parents to attend Sunday school, and I remember how I was trying to get out of attending more than participating and I always wanted to play. Most of the day was devoted to church services. Sunday school started at 9 am, followed by church service at 10:30 am, 1:30 pm, 2 pm, and 7:30 pm. The youth service was at 6 pm.

I later taught Junior Class in Sunday School, and I remember the requirements for the students in addition to the text: to learn and repeat the Lord's prayer, the 23rd Psalm, the 13th chapter of the Corinthians, the Beatitudes, Spiritual Gifts, Fruits of the Spirit and the Books of the Bible. Sunday school was a strong influence in transmitting values on morality, what to do and what not to do, and how to know what was right and what was wrong. In addition, Sunday school also fostered pride in our culture by sponsoring inter-church competitions among different classes every 5th Sunday in alternating locations by reciting bible scriptures, poetry, singing, or playing musical instruments.

A memorable influence was the music contribution of Rosa Stratton. She was a pianist who taught piano and music in her home and was highly regarded in the community, and her students became many of the church musicians. My mother knew how to play the piano and occasionally would volunteer as the accompanist in church and she wanted us to learn and enrolled us with Mrs. Rosa. Alas, I couldn't tell one tune from another and spent my time with her avoiding my lessons. My sister Jennie became the family pianist instead.

I was very impressionable as a young child and there were three church members that held me in awe: Reverend Cook, Mr. Charles Bragg, and Reverend Campbell.

Reverend Cook was our neighbor on Jefferson Ave, and I loved hanging out with him. He allowed me to observe him make a concoction of herbs and medicinal ingredients that he'd prepare into an inhalant. He would breathe the fumes to relieve his bronchial condition. I thought it was cool and I remember thinking I'd like to do that one day. It was not so much the substance use I wanted to experience, but the special relationship of intimacy and secrecy that characterized my identification with the activity.

Mr. Charles Bragg was a church volunteer who'd come out early in the morning to ring the church bells. I was fascinated by the bells and I was up early as was the custom was with my parents and none of the kids would be up at that time yet, so I'd be there in the belfry with Mr. Bragg and he'd let me ring the bells. I was little then and the bells were heavy, and I had to hang to the ropes with all my weight and jump up and down to ring the bells, but it was glorious once I accomplished the task.

Another I admired was the Reverend Campbell, he was the only minister I knew then who went to the university and had a Master's in Divinity. I thought he was intellectual and very learned, which influenced my determination to go to college later.

After the Revolution, the Anglican Church lost state support and congregation and succumbed to the general reformation movement sweeping England and Europe. The Episcopal Church was its transformation, but on the Eastern Shore new religions and churches were rapidly spreading and brought about by charismatic evangelical preachers. First came the Baptists, then the Methodists, Quakers, and Presbyterians.

Methodism quickly spread to be the dominant new church on the shore and one famous preacher then was a Freedman who assisted Francis

Asbury, the itinerant preacher on horseback who traveled the Eastern Shore nurturing the struggling Methodist movement, as his travel companion, valet, and groom. "Black Harry" Hosier, who was born a slave in North Carolina, and somehow obtained or was granted his freedom, and despite being illiterate, developed remarkable preaching skills and possessing a photographic memory meant he could repeat hymns and texts with great accuracy. He began preaching to Blacks who came to hear Asbury speak and later to Whites who stayed on to experience the novelty of a Black preacher. Later on, he was assistant to Thomas Coke, who was sent from England to organize the separate Methodist congregations into a separate independent American church.

With Asbury going north and Harry and Coke going south into the Delmarva peninsula, soon "Black Harry" was attracting overflow crowds to hear him preach. For two decades Harry worked side by side with these two White bishops together with another Black preacher, Richard Allen, who tried to teach Harry how to read and write, but Harry gave up the effort after he found out that it constricted his freedom of expression. Methodists began as an inclusive church and espoused an anti-slavery philosophy, but it changed later and after Harry's death, Richard Allen separated from the denomination and established the African Methodist Episcopal (AME) Church on the Eastern Shore. The era of religious equality had ended, and churches began adding back galleries in the churches, separating Black worshippers from Whites.

After the Civil War, newly freed Blacks who couldn't worship with Whites in established churches began to build their own churches, and it was in this setting where the idea of organizing to end segregation took root. The Black church gave birth to charismatic preachers who transcended the color difference.

Leonard Treherne was born free having had a free mother and a slave father owned by Curtis Treherne in Shady Side near Machipongo. His mother's father, Lyttleton G. Church was the largest Black farmer in Northampton and Accomack counties. He had a career as a political appointee after Reconstruction, then was ordained and became pastor of The Ebenezer and Antioch Baptist Church.

Jimmy Cliff founded the Jerusalem Baptist Church in Temperanceville. He was a former slave who served in the A Company, Regiment 1 EV Infantry during the Civil War.

After the Civil War, several Black Baptists escaped to Philadelphia from the Eastern Shore, and no other congregation would admit them except the First Baptist Church. The First African Baptist Church grew out of this congregation through the efforts of Caleb James Burris, who was born a slave at Kendall Grove, near Eastvale. Convinced he was born to preach, he persuaded his owner, Robert S. Costin, to permit him to travel to Philadelphia to work to purchase his freedom. He only obtained his master's consent when two of his cousins, free men Samuel and John Bibbins, placed themselves in bondage as security. After a year, he saved enough money to buy his freedom and release his cousins from bondage, who then helped him in his ministry. He became the founder and first pastor of the Union Baptist Church in Eastville, and the first African-American ordained minister to serve in Virginia Eastern Shore.

Thomas Nelson Baker, who was born on the Nottingham Plantation in Eastville, of enslaved parents, was the first African-American born a slave who received his Ph.D. in Philosophy from Yale, preached in his sermons that African-Americans needed to define their own identity as a people rather than assume the identity perpetuated by the dominant White culture, at the Second Congregational Church in Pittsville, Massachusetts, where he served as pastor for thirty-eight years.

During the Jim Crow Era, the only woman minister from the Eastern Shore Reverend Mary D. Upshur was a member of the Union Baptist Church in Eastvale, attended seminary in Lynchburg, Virginia and preached at some of the largest congregations on the East Coast, from Atlantic City, New Jersey, Philadelphia, Pennsylvania, Baltimore, Maryland.

As important is the influence of these Black ministers in the role of Black churches in organizing against slavery after the revolution, after the Civil War, and during the civil protest era, until Kirk Mariner's "Revival's Children", there is very little written about the work of these religious leaders on the Eastern Shore, part of the glaring omission of the Black thread in weaving the fabric of history, especially in Cape Charles.

I continued to attend the First Baptist Church until I began to have a sense of dissatisfaction about how my life was going. I have gone through many ups and downs since before and after my marriage, I have done so much and had many more experiences than most people my age, yet I felt unfulfilled, I felt empty, my life was running on neutral, something was missing.

I was smoking and drinking, and I worried that it may become a problem in fulfilling my job. I am a mortician and could be called at any time of day or night, I wondered what families would think if I answered a call and they smelled alcohol on me. My father was someone who instilled pride in his work, he was a perfectionist who demanded the highest standards and quality in any job. I found myself applying this in my work but would often feel frustrated with my results. I needed to find a way to accept these frustrations but felt that I have not given this task all my effort so I could accept the limits of my ability.

I was going to church and felt I needed to do something more than pay lip service, and that I hadn't touched the Holy Spirit and all of its splendor and the miracles yet to be seen. I sought God even as I served Him. I felt I was at a crossroad and I began searching with greater curiosity and zeal, it was robust. I was in this state one night sitting in my living room at 543 Jefferson Ave with a beer in hand, feeling overwhelmed and I yelled," God, come!! Take this away from me," and I pushed from the chair and hurled the beer to the floor.

Juanita seeing my agitated state and thinking perhaps that she should leave this deranged man alone, took the children upstairs to the bedroom, but as soon as they left, I beheld this bright light fill the room and engulfed me in its glow. I have never witnessed such bright light before and I was paralyzed, I couldn't move, I only wished that Juanita had not left so she could witness it too. For several days, I had experienced this intermittently and I felt I was being led around the world as if no one else was around me. I tried to make a phone call but I couldn't remember the number. I felt there was some force controlling me like my life was on a roller coaster. I went to my pastor for consultation and he gave me a book to read from his library. God was directing my path; this was when the Holy Spirit became my guide. That was my revelation and I began to hear a voice.

"Come out from amongst ye," said the voice as I passed a certain church. I sensed that He wanted me to leave my church and seek a new one, but I wasn't clear as to which church to join. I ignored the voice. I couldn't understand why I was being guided to leave my church since my family had been going to the First Baptist church on Nectarine and Madison since my grandparent's days and I was happy there. I had taught Sunday school there and I had an important role as a trustee, so I ignored the voice for several months.

However, I started to attend Sunday services from different churches to determine what church I should change to. I even attended different churches while I was visiting Detroit and Florida. I'd hear the voice more clearly and sometimes the voice would be a thought that didn't feel like it was my own but inserted in my mind, other times it would be a distinct speaking voice I'd hear outside of my head like I would hear from another person, and later as I repeated the experience, I could tell more readily it was the voice of God.

Meanwhile, I was spending more time doing work for the church at Fairview, the Mt. Sinai Gospel Tabernacle. They asked me for help in renovating the church and I did volunteer work doing the electrical upgrade and doing some framing and other construction jobs. I also helped in saving them money by showing them how they were being exploited by a heating/AC firm, which had been overcharging them for inadequate service. For several months, I was doing some work in this church and attending Sunday services. I continued to feel the Holy Spirit guiding me and my faith was strengthened by many manifestations of its presence. By praying deeply and having profound faith, I could lay my hands on the sick and through the power of the Holy Spirit guiding me they could become well, or I could pray for rain or sunshine and it would come to pass. I prayed over Juanita to heal her burns when she accidentally held her hand over the stove and it healed with hardly any scar or pain.

I also accepted the gift of my ability to exorcise the devil from those who were possessed. I have been called by neighbors to help a member who was extremely agitated, out of control, thrashing about, breaking things, and destroying the house. Police had even been called to subdue the man, but the family also called me and when I came, I knew that the devil was in possession of the man. I called him out and commanded that he leaves, and I felt the power of the Holy Spirit drive the demon away.

On another occasion, I confronted a man who was acting in a deranged manner and was choking his mother. I confronted the devil and commanded him to leave. Another involved a family member, who was acting bizarre, going about the house covering windows and putting a towel over the TV believing that the devil was controlling her from the TV and lurking outside. I didn't realize it, but I called her Margie instead of her name, Marge, and she responded not in a voice coming from her mouth but in one coming from somewhere out of her chest. When I called her Margie again, she became more agitated and I knew that Margie was the devil and I commanded her to leave.

The Holy Spirit has the power to exorcise, and I am his instrument to do it and I accept that as a blessing. I have felt the power protect me from several near-death experiences even before I had accepted the Spirit to guide my life, which was so profound and sublime and strengthened my faith deeply. For example, I once felt a hand snatch me from falling to my death while working with my father on a construction site, and another time I was saved from being crushed to death by a rolling stone by a timely intervention that stopped the stone's momentum.

Almost two years later I passed the Mt. Sinai Gospel Tabernacle again and I heard God's Voice, "Come out from amongst ye." I had ignored this, but then I heard God say, "Did I not tell you?"

And I knew that the Holy Spirit guided me to join the Mt. Sinai Gospel Tabernacle because they needed help the most, and I could fulfill the Holy Spirit's work of service to others most in this church. And I was able to leave the First Baptist Church, and today I've been a member of the Tabernacle for over twenty years and my wife Juanita worships with me and found her gift as a minister. I found support in the Tabernacle in the way I experience my faith, and they accepted my gifts of laying of hands and exorcism of the devil.

I found fulfillment in my ability to serve those who need help and they in turn help me in fulfilling my obligation to serve God. With my faith, I can deal with all the adversity and injustices I suffered without being consumed by anger and the need for retribution. I believe God dealt with those who had been evil in the way their fortunes have been lost or in the way they had experienced negative events, such as death or illness. I continue to pray and feel the Holy Spirit within me although I do not heed its voice sometimes and allow myself to listen to the devil, I know when not to let the devil tell me and instead follow the command of the Holy Spirit. I have followed its guidance in behaving according to God's commandments especially in my relationship with my wife, by not committing adultery, and with others by not taking from them.

At this point in my life, I continue to feel the Holy Spirit and it guided me into finding the help I needed to share my experience of growing up a grandson of a slave, and navigating the indignities of segregation and overcoming obstacles of systemic racism to become the first Black elected official to the Cape Charles City Council, and to the Board of Supervisors of Northampton County. It guided me to tell my story so that others may keep hope that through faith one could live a life of fulfillment by serving God.

First Baptist Church

# Chapter 12: I am Who I am

Thirty years ago, when I was fifty-two, I received a surprise letter from Rachel, who was in 7th grade at Huntington Middle School in Newport News. She was in the academic Excel program and on the honor roll and would like to be a lawyer when she grew up. She was writing as part of her assignment in Language Arts, a friendly note telling me about herself and in turn, asking me about myself and what my dreams were. I answered her and kept a copy of the rough draft and I thought it was interesting to review what I shared with her at that time to evaluate whether I have come to live my dreams or whether I am still dreaming.

"My dream is to bring the whole world closer to me, mentally. This is to be achieved by travel, reading, and meeting many people. I find it interesting to meet people with different mores and diversified backgrounds. The heritage of the various races and historical data and their contribution seems to be provocative to me."

Those were a lot of words for a thirteen-year-old to process, so I didn't know how she handled that. But the practical advice that I gave her was taught to me by my parents. I wrote:

"If I thought I could have adequate advice to give someone today, it would be to explore as many occupations as I could and give careful consideration to their qualifications and actual direction of their mission. Then, select one or two that I would be happy with for the rest of my life. In addition, I advise you to think before you speak and act but speak up and out when necessary. Always remember this: God gave you a good start with a clean body that is like a temple, and it will reward you in the future."

I was busy with tasks and acted on opportunities that were presented to me. I've tried a hundred occupations since I was six years old, from running errands for my father, to cutting grass, washing cars, driving, newspaper delivery, cement contracting, electrician, politician, civic and community organizing, volunteer, and funeral director. In these various occupations, I got to meet many people from different backgrounds, and they got to know me. I traveled with my older son to Bermuda; visited my daughter in West Palm Beach, North Carolina, and Washington, DC; went to college in Richmond and Philadelphia. I participated in sit-ins and protests during the Civil Rights Movement. I married my high school sweetheart and became a father and grandfather. I buried parents and a son too soon, and now my wife and I are caring for our ailing and aging siblings. I celebrated my eighty-second birthday on March 2, 2020, and I thank God for having survived the Covid-19 pandemic, and growing old with my wife who, like me, is eighty-two.

My grandmother lived to be 84 years old and my mother to 101. I feel I have many more years ahead of me. I am still operating Gray's Funeral Home and continue to be involved in various civic organizations. I hope I made some difference in the people who came to me for help and helped in moving the struggle for social equality forward, for the struggle continues even today, with the nation-wide protest going on in the death of George Floyd at the hands of police and the president's overreaction by calling in the military to break up the mostly peaceful protest crowd.

The news broadcast brings memories that I have long kept unexamined, but couldn't suppress any longer. My younger son had been dealing with a drinking problem that was distressing to me and made me feel impotent, but how he was treated by my community here in Cape Charles, I feel, had no justification and I will not be silent any longer. I shudder to think that my son could have been easily a victim like George Floyd if he wasn't so out of it in this incident which I recall with great anxiety and fear.

I was called by a friend to come and intervene when she found out that the commotion on Mason Avenue that day involved my son, who was thrown out into the street from a bar very drunk. He was so drunk that all he could do was to stagger to the police car and sit in a semi-stupor in the back seat. Soon, the street was blocked off and swarming with the sheriff and state police vehicles in response to my son's drunkenness who was not aggressive or behaving violently at all but was rather helpless in his drunken stupor.

I came after being summoned by my friend, but the whole scene had dispersed by the time I got there, but it was intimidating to have a full out police response to a drunken man. However, the police did not see the need to make any other arrests, not even the proprietor of the establishment, who shouldn't have served my son after having had too many drinks. Why I didn't do anything and go into the bar to determine what exactly happened and press charges was because I am Black and would not get anywhere with confronting this directly. This had been a pattern here in my "idyllic" community of Cape Charles.

In contrast, I observed a White man driving recklessly who appeared quite drunk and hit a mailbox. One policeman came and talked with the man first, and then had him ride with him in his police vehicle. No handcuffs or any show of forceful police authority.

I had a recent incident where I stopped to offer my help to a White woman who appeared to be having some trouble and was stopped on the side of the road. The woman rejected my offer of help and nervously waved me away as a policeman came to see what was going on. I was immediately asked to leave by the policeman. I knew these situations well and I felt threatened. My response was to comply without trying to find out exactly what was going on, for instinctively I knew that my being Black would open the incident to misinterpretation of my action and lead to potential violence. If I asked to know the reason why, I would be viewed as arguing and may be arrested. The officer would escalate his use of authority until violence erupted.

And yet, these young Black men who did not experience the era of Jim Crow, behaved like any person would. They ask questions and look the policeman directly in the eye for an answer. Their behavior could be judged as insolent and aggressive and would be used to justify police violence. It is scary for a young Black man to be headstrong and question why he was being stopped by the police, for he will be responded to with the full force of authority without any insight that his behavior is just how most young men would behave. Because he is Black, though, his behavior is interpreted as resistance and aggression and that justifies a full application of police authority.

It is indeed scary to be Black in America, and our children still have to be mindful of the Black Code in order to survive. When will the season be right for change? My grandmother who was a slave lived to be 84 years old and legally was free, but true equality remained elusive at her death in 1938 and it remains unrealized in my time, 82 years later.

# Epilogue

It was a special journey for me to write this book and to get to know Tom Godwin. Before this, my knowledge about slavery and racism was based on the history classes in high school which were taught in the Philippines by memorizing dates and forgotten after final exams. When I joined the exodus to the US after medical school graduation in 1967, my knowledge of the US was shaped by movies, Elvis and Pat Boone, Coca Cola, blue jeans, and the Sears Roebuck catalog.

I remember the giddy feeling I'd have whenever my mother's order from Sears would arrive. I loved showing off my stateside things and I especially treasured the doll that I shared with my sisters. It had blond hair that you could comb and style in any fashion and it provided us with hours of pleasure. It even had moving blue eyes that looked real and would close to sleep whenever you lay it down and it had a baby cry when you tilted it a certain way.

Everything that my mother ordered from the Sears pages was special and no one else among my friends had anything like them, and so my impression of the US was set along this parameter of popular culture, media advertising, and consumerism. I thought I'd like to live a life of adventure like Nancy Drew and the Hardy Boys, and I loved the movies of Doris Day, James Dean, and Rock Hudson. The vision of living the American dream for me and my friends filled our imagination and it never occurred to us that we would experience racism, but we didn't look at it in that context at first.

But consciousness about race began with our application for immigration. We didn't know how to classify ourselves. We didn't fit any of the categories: Black, White, American Indian/Alaskan Native,

Asian American, or Hawaiian/Pacific Islander. As a Filipino, I didn't fit into any of these classifications. Many of us checked White, but our experience, later on, showed us that in the US we were considered Black.

In our first year, we bought cars and was in awe that we could get one on $50 down payment and the rest on credit. That was truly a culture shock. In the Philippines we bought everything on a cash basis, to have debt would be embarrassing whereas here to have debt is a way to prove your fiduciary trustworthiness. We were excited to take our vacation visiting friends in other states to show off our new Camaros or Mustangs. A friend driving through North Carolina couldn't understand why he couldn't purchase milk for his child from the main entrance of a convenience store. From the front counter, he was shooed to the Colored area. Another woke up with a burning cross in his yard after they moved into their house in a subdivision in Clayton County, Georgia. Another friend had to marry his American fiancée in another state because, in Georgia, mixed marriage was illegal.

I never had to be conscious about my color before, but on further examination after being thrown off balance by the census' racial categories and my initial confusion at being treated as a Black person, I realized Filipinos are very much influenced by the experience of more than 300 years of Spanish colonization. The effect of colonial subjugation and oppression on individual and group identity was very similar to the effects of slavery and its legacy remains as powerful drivers of our self-representation and attitudes today. When the Stockholm Syndrome was popularized in the 1970s, after a psychological phenomenon described by Swedish psychiatrists who treated the bank hostages for post-traumatic symptoms after their release, it gave me the tool to conceptualize what colonial mentality and racism were.

The Stockholm Syndrome, a psychological phenomenon used to describe the sympathetic and bonding behavior of hostages to their captors can be applied to colonial mentality and racism as the societal expression of this bonding behavior. The elements are satisfied by the characteristics of both Spanish imperialism in the Philippines and slavery in the US. The captor is all-powerful in reality and there is little hope for resistance. The survival of the captive is dependent on the little kindnesses and benevolence of the captor and the ability of the captive to please his captor. The captive is isolated from other influences by preventing him from learning and keeping the captive illiterate. There is a suppression of indigenous ways by forcible conversion to Christianity and, over time, the captives begin to adopt the captor's ways as the better way since it is equated with survival, eventually seeing their ways and own characteristics as inferior.

This ultimately extends along racial and genetic lines as the supreme way of identifying or being like the captor. In the Philippines, this is demonstrated in the ever-increasing preoccupation with achieving Caucasian characteristics by the proliferation of skin lightening products and cosmetic surgery. In the Philippines, it seems that to be like a Spaniard in looks, privilege, association, upbringing, education, manner, and pedigree is the ultimate pride. Who is the Filipino mother who did not inspect the color of her baby's skin at birth and the shape of its nose, to see if it looks like a Spaniard, fair and aquiline, and beamed with pride? To associate with mestizos, to speak Spanish, and be accepted is a mark of belonging. Even the bastard children of Spanish descended liaisons carry this aura.

We speak of colonial mentality, and how this keeps Filipinos in the bottom of progress and national pride among its Asian neighbors. One must be aware of this thinking and must always be alert to its negative and oppressive forces. It saps creative energy. It shares survival dynamics with traumatized, terrorized, or victimized groups.

It is unfortunate that the Philippines, when Spain colonized it in 1565, was a disparate land of unorganized small tribes, with none dominating to unite the archipelago into one kingdom. We were not a nation nor a culture. We were a collection of regional tribes, to which we identify our allegiance even to this day. Hence, we see ourselves more clearly as Ilocanos, Tagalogs, Bicolanos, Visayan, etc., rather than Filipino. We compete with each other and undermine each other as part of this tribal one-upmanship.

The Spaniards put us under one rule and made us a nation, and as a nation, we adopted the colonial identity which we carry to this day. We are still trying to be like a Spaniard, the Filipino is still the Indio, and the Filipino-American? He is living the American dream, Hollywood style, all show, no substance, for he exists still as an outsider, and his color and ethnic looks in White racist America continue to remind him that he is different in an inferior kind of way. Many individuals, of course, have crossed the threshold among his friends and those who know him, but until that happens, the Filipino-American is judged in and around the developed world by the color of his skin and by the height of his nose.

Colonial mentality is akin to racism, it assumes that one group, the enslaver, is inherently superior and dominates the inferior group, the enslaved, and it is entrenched in the system that governs these groups.

I'll illustrate how I conceptualize the Stockholm Syndrome to understand racism. The dynamic is free-flowing, for the enslaver-enslaved roles interact with each other and influence each another. It shares dynamics with survival instinct and post-traumatic stress syndrome of survivors of wars, torture, kidnapping, abuse, and forcible separations.

The enslaver is all-powerful in reality and there is little hope in the enslaved for resistance. This must be continually maintained by the White enslaver by ever-increasing cruelty, and by systemic laws that control the behavior of the enslaved, so he will remain subjugated. If the enslaved rebels, there are punishments that quickly reestablish the power of the enslaver. This is achieved by passing laws among which were in the Black Code laws, the Law of 1806, and the Jim Crow Laws after reconstruction in 1877.

The survival of the enslaved is dependent on the little kindnesses and benevolence of the enslaver and the ability of the enslaved to please his enslaver. This happens when little favors are given that make the enslaved feel special, such as the experience of Candis Godwin who wore the hand-me-down clothing of her enslaver's children that is so much finer than slave clothing and by being taken from field labor to be a house slave and the children's playmate.

In turn, the enslaved develops vigilance into the enslaver's wishes, desires, and moods so he can please his enslaver with the expectation of lenient treatment and perhaps of survival itself. Hence, we see slaves who are obsequious in order to keep the arc complete in the conferring of more little acts of kindness and pleasing behaviors to the extent that the slave will give up his life for his master if called upon.

The enslaved is isolated from other influences by preventing him from learning and keeping him illiterate. There is a prohibition on education, and any knowledge that the slave has is provided by the master, so that his world view is defined by the master's views, developing dependency which prevents the slave from leaving.

There is a suppression of indigenous ways by forcible conversion to Christianity. This effectively erases the enslave's past and facilitates his adoption of the master's culture and beliefs. This wreaks havoc in how one views oneself, especially in the disorientation produced by being transported from one's place of birth, to another completely alien environment. One's sense of self is annihilated in the loss of everything associated with his being; the loss of kinship with others who could reflect his image to him. He is stripped of his clothes, his name, his language, his values, and his beliefs, he becomes an empty shell to be bombarded with the enslaver's intrusions into his psyche.

Over time, the enslaved begins to adopt the enslaver's ways as the better way since it is equated with survival, eventually seeing his ways and own characteristics as inferior. An example is seen in the preoccupation to have straight hair like the enslaver's, and denigrating his tufted, tightly curled hair as undesirable.

This ultimately extends along genetic lines as the supreme way of identifying or being like the enslaver. This, of course, was abhorrent to Whites as they believed in the superiority of the race and fearful of diluting it by miscegenation.

Slavery as an institution is woven tightly in the psyche of Americans both Black and White, but it is not incorporated in the day-to-day awareness of everyone. Rather, it is viewed as separate and given attention by special events or special citations.

Whenever I attended any lecture or event that promoted racial awareness, the presenters and majority of the audience are Black. Blacks have been aware of how slavery has affected their identity, and we have seen the movements to correct these like the Black is Beautiful campaign, and of course, the Civil Rights Movement, and recently the Black Lives Matter Movement.

It appears to me that if anyone needs to be aware of racism, it should be Whites who need to go and attend and learn from these meetings, for they are the originators and beneficiaries of the system of slavery and therefore have continuing vested interest in perpetuating these racist attitudes. Until they begin to accept this role, they will continue to invent rationalizations to promote racism in the laws they pass, in the way they hire or promote workers, in the way they build housing, the way they fund schools, select books and award scholarships, in the way they present Blacks in the media, movies, and entertainment, in the way they limit opportunity for social equality and the pursuit of happiness.

Early on, Blacks have adopted education as a way to improve their competitive ability and they have pushed for legislation to remove racism in the laws, but racism continues in the hearts of everyone. It is ingrained in the culture, absorbed like water seeping into the roots, sustaining life itself.

It seems to me that there is no way for true equality to exist unless, Whites acknowledge that unchecked White privilege maintains racism by keeping Blacks from competing fairly, and it will take more than a generation to equalize the disparity in all areas of competition before Blacks can catch up. Also Blacks need to be aware of how centuries of being considered property and at the mercy for survival of his White owners have affected his view of himself and his place in the world and how this is expressed in his current adaptation. Both races should be aware of how their actions continue to maintain the dynamics of the enslaver/enslaved relationship and how vigilance in changing these patterns is the key to developing true equality of the races. The expectation that Blacks should be on their way without systemic protection and support is unrealistic and unfair, for like in golf, one must play with a handicap to truly be competitive, otherwise without hope of winning, it will be futile to play the game.

Our Monroe Avenue Home

# Acknowledgments

By Tom Godwin:

Lee Banks, my architect friend, who inspired me to build my house on Monroe Avenue, sooner than I had planned

Mayor George Ward, whose significant influence enabled me to secure the property for my home.

Minerva Meacham, for her encouragement and support in helping me enter the political arena.

Edith Mitchell, for inspiring the youth of Cape Charles to get involved in my campaigns for a seat in the Cape Charles City Council and in the Board of Supervisors of Northampton County

My wife and family for their constant support.



By Metty Vargas Pellicer, Author:

I am indebted to Tom for his candor and openness in sharing his story and to Juanita, his wife for her complete support of this project by helping Tom remember.

I am grateful to Mary M. Barrow, award-winning author of "Small Moments, A Child's Memories of the Civil Rights Movement" and mentor of Expressions, Eastern Shore Writers Group, for her encouragement and valuable feedback and her belief in the importance of this book by her generous monetary donation towards its publication and to Expressions Writing Group members, for their support and feedback.

To Marion Naar, Board Member of the Cape Charles Museum, for her helpful suggestions and knowledge about historical resources, I am deeply appreciative.

To Miles Barnes, retired Librarian of the Eastern Shore Library and historian, for his support and valuable historical input.

To Leslie Arambulo, my editor and my sister Minda for technical services in preparing the manuscript for publication.

To Diane Dawson, Linda Schulz and all readers of the manuscript before publication for their feedback and review.

To all the folks at booklocker.com, publisher, for their professionalism and efficiency.

I have used the following books for reference and found Kirk Mariner's books especially informative and fascinating. I could not cite specific references in the book as I was pretty informal in utilizing the information I learned and this information I weave freely in the book. I strive to be accurate in citing historical data and checked them against these sources:

Dickon, Chris, "Eastern Shore Railroad", Arcadia Publishing, Charleston, SC 2006

Hess, Ann M., "The Bridgetown Files", Home School Project, 2014

Hurston, Zora Neale, "Barracoon, The Story of the Last Black Cargo", Harper Collins Publishers, NY 2018

Hurston, Zora Neale, "Their Eyes Were Watching God", Harper and Row Publishers 1990

Johnson, William H. "Memoirs of an Eastern Shore Physician", Hickory House, Eastville, VA 23347

Lattimer, Frances Bibbins. "Life for Me Ain't Been No Crystal Stair", George Lattimer, Eastville, VA 23347

Lattimer, Frances Bibbins, "The Journey of a Multiracial Family", Hickory House, Eastville VA 23347

Lewis, Jim, "Cape Charles: A Railroad Town", Hickory House, Eastville, Virginia, VA 23347

Mariner, Kirk, "Glimpses of a Vanished Eastern Shore", Miona Publications, Onancock, VA 23417

Mariner, Kirk, "Slave and Free, On Virginia's Eastern Shore", Miona Publications, Onancock, VA 23417

Mariner, Kirk, "Off 13, The Eastern Shore of VA Guidebook", Miona Publications, Onancock, VA, Publications 23417

Mariner, Kirk, "True Tales of the Eastern Shore", Miona Publications, Onancock VA 23417

Rimington, Karen Godwin, "Who Was John Wesley Godwin?", Pamphlet

Schulz, Linda, PhD., Editor, Rosenwald School Restoration Initiative, "The Heart of a Community", Pamphlet supported by a Grant from the Virginia Humanities 2019

Tyson, Timothy B., "The Blood of Emmett Till", Simon and Schuster Paperbacks NY London Toronto Sydney New Delhi

Warren, John, "Chesapeake Bay Bridge-Tunnel", Arcadia Publishing, Charleston, SC 2015

I also used Google search extensively, and these websites were worth bookmarking:

https://www.loc.gov/item/mesn170/

https://www.ferris.edu/HTMLS/news/jimcrow/

https://www.history.com/topics/american-civil-war/reconstruction

http://afrovirginia.org/items/show/420

https://www.meaningfulfunerals.net/stories

https://capecharleswave.com/2014/01/oral-history-a-chat-with-alston-godwin/

https://capecharleswave.com/2013/01/alston-joynes-godwin-101-pioneer-female-undertaker/

https://capecharles.municipalcms.com//files/documents/job4821469100114112132a.pdf

https://www.13newsnow.com/article/news/history/cape-charles-exhibit-highlights-segregation-era-school/291-553029662

https://www.delmarvanow.com/story/news/local/virginia/2016/05/16/play-depicts-stronger-than-steel-va-shore-women/84274346/

https://virginiahumanities.org/2017/03/from-the-archives-to-the-stage/

https://kpeasternshore.wordpress.com/tag/stronger-than-steel/

http://www.capecharlesmirror.com/news/cape-charles-historical-society-exhibition-stronger-than-steel-four-women-four-years-one-war/

# Photos

Grandma Joynes at her farm tending to the chickens

The Cape Charles Museum

The pavilion

Jefferson avenue

# Tom Godwin: Curriculum Vitae

**Thomas George Godwin**

DOB March 2, 1938

Cape Charles, VA 23310

**Married** to: Juanita Brickhouse Godwin November 15, 1960

Children

Keith Ansel April 12,1961- August 13, 2011 (deceased)

Tommy 1969

Tonja 1970

Grandchildren

Glenn, Jr.

Madison

**Education:**

Cape Charles School Grades 1-7, Graduated 1952

Northampton County High School Machining, VA Grades 8-12, Graduated 1955

Virginia Union University Richmond, VA Graduated 1958

Mortician Apprenticeship, Thomas Funeral Home, Accomack, VA, 1958-1960

Eckels College of Mortuary Science, Philadelphia PA, Graduated 1961

**Director and Owner,** Gray's Funeral Home, 3rd Generation proprietor of the first Black-owned Funeral Home on the Eastern Shore established in 1895

**Elected Offices and Board Appointments**

Cape Charles City Council Board Member

1980-1990 Northampton County Board of Supervisors

Chairman, 1990

Northampton County School Board, Chairman

Northampton-Accomack Board of Transportation

1984-1987 President Northampton- Accomack Housing Board

1980-1992 Member Northampton-Accomack Housing Board

1988-1991-Northampton County Commission on Tourism Board

Northampton Small Business Board

1987 Northampton County Social Services Board

Northampton County Senior Center

Northampton County Health Department Sanitarian

Northampton County Boy Scouts

Virginia Beach Board, Gubernatorial Appointment

1986-1991 Selective Service Draft Board, Chairman and Secretary

Cape Charles Concerned Citizens Association, Chairman

Cape Charles Chamber of Commerce, Vice President, and Treasurer

Cheriton Senior Citizen Center, Founder, and Chairman

Black Elected Officials Association (The Black Caucus) Charter Member

Cape Charles Library Board

Cape Charles Little League

Cape Charles Fire Marshall

**Professional Affiliations**

Norfolk Funeral Directors Association, President

Virginia Funeral Directors Association

100 Black Women Funeral Directors, Honored as 50-year professional

**Civic Associations Affiliations**

Cape Charles Rotary Club

Northampton County High School Alumni Association

Northampton County NAACP

Mt. Sinai Gospel Tabernacle, Deacon

Cape Charles First Baptist, Trustee

Prince Hall Masonic Lodge, District Deputy Grand Master

Prince Hall Affiliated Masonic Lodge, Royal Arch Degree

Valentin Lodge #83, Master

Peninsula Lodge #127, Master

**Awards, Recognitions, Honors**

First Black Elected Official Member of the Cape Charles Town Council and the Northampton County Board of Supervisors, with a landslide victory

Chairman, Northampton County Board of Supervisors

Gubernatorial Appointee to the Virginia Beach Board by Governors Baliles, Holton and Wilder

Senatorial Appointee by Senator Bloxom

Founder and Chairman of the Cheriton Senior Center

Integrated the Northampton County Golf Club, by gaining membership

Appointed the first Black woman to the Northampton Housing Board

while serving as Chairman

Supported the election of the first Black woman Mayor of Cape Charles

Instituted prayer at the beginning of meetings of the Virginia Beach Board

September 14, 2008-Recipient "Distinguished Man of the Eastern Shore," by Gaskins Chapel African Methodist Episcopal Church

February 25, 2018-Speaker, "Cape Charles, The African-American Community Back in the Day," African Baptist Church celebration of Black History of the Eastern Shore

May 11, 2019-Story-Teller, "A Cape Charles Century, Past, Present, and Future," presented at the historic Palace Theater on the 100th Anniversary of Cape Charles Library

At corner of Bay and Mason Avenue

# About the Author

Metty Vargas Pellicer aka Metty Pellicer, Metty Vargas, Fiameta Vargas, Fiameta Pellicer, Fiameta Vargas Pellicer, is a grandmother, mother, woman, and doctor. She was born in the Philippines in 1942 and immigrated to the US in 1967 after graduating from the University of the Philippines College of Medicine. She was married to John Pellicer for 35 years until his death in 2004 from coronary heart disease at age 58. English is a second language and she speaks two of the Filipino dialects, Tagalog and Bicolano, *y un poquito Espanol.* She has published two books, "Hello, From Somewhere: Stories of the Roads I Traveled" and "From Miman, With Love: A Grandmother's Memoir".

She moved to Cape Charles, VA in 2017 and is happy in her retirement with new friends, travel, exploring the rich history of the Eastern Shore, writing, and gardening. Her books can be purchased at:

https://booklocker.com/books/7848.html

at her website- https://mettypellicer.com

or at

https://www.amazon.com/Metty-Pellicer/e/B00RS0JS3U?ref_=dbs_p_ebk_r00_abau_000000